Nothing on heaven or earth can be
Likened to a person who has decided
To allow Holiness to enter in.

God's Holy Spirit

The Final Frontier
The Seamless Space of Heaven

Gerald E. Collins

Requests for permission should be addressed to:
Gerald E. Collins
https://geraldcollins.com

Cover Design by Reflections Publishing House and Clark Graphics

ISBN 978-0-9965296-3-1
Library of Congress Control Number 2015945287
First Printing, July 2016

Reflections Publishing House
Inglewood, CA
https://reflectph.com

Books by Gerald E. Collins

The Only Life Worth Living
Healing the Sense of Separation
Restoring Wholeness
A Book of Spiritual Practices

Love's Magic
A series of Short Stories about
Mystics and their Relationships with God

Passion, Power, and Peace
A Magical Love Story of
Passion and Conquests

Raise Beautiful Children
A Spiritual Parenting Guide to
Bringing Forth the Incredible

Deceit
Romance, Deception, Compromise
Amid Elegance and Desire

TABLE OF CONTENTS

For ye shall go out with joy, and be led forth
with peace: the mountains and the hills shall
break forth before you into singing, and all the
trees of the field shall clap their hands.
Isaiah 55:12

Acknowledgments

Must acknowledge family especially my four siblings for their support as I worked diligently to complete this project. Sharon, Steven, Victor, and Carol have been very supportive as they may have wondered what I was doing. Thank God for their support.

Also want to acknowledge my wonderful wife JV for her understanding during this period.

Bill Stroup, Wendy Taylor and the practitioners at Agape also provided the consciousness to support production of this document.

All those at Reflections Publishing including Debbie Bellis have done their job well.

Foreword

In this worldly experience that we're having here on planet earth, there truly is only one "problem" and it shows up in an endless variety of ways. The one and only challenge that we ever have is that we believe that we are separate from the Divine. When we're broke we feel separate from abundance. When our loved one leaves us we feel separate from love. When we're too fat or too thin we feel separate from beauty, from fitting in and feeling worthy. Over and over again, the one thought of separation shows up to create a "problem."

Through this writing Gerald E. Collins helps us to remember that the appearance of separation is not true and it never will be true no matter how thoroughly convinced we are of separation. We cannot separate ourselves from the whole of God. We are part of the infinite Holiness and ever shall we be.

Walking this journey of awakening, we have a friend who can never leave us. I call it the Holy Higher Spirit Self, or the Holy Self, or the Higher Self or the Holy Spirit. Some call it the I AM Presence. Whatever we call it, it is there for us to call upon, 24/7.

This Holy Spirit is that Divine Partner that we've all been searching for. It is the wise one that we can depend upon. And it is this partnership that is the great healer.

Like all of the Master Teachers, Gerald reminds us to get into that partnership, and to be in relationship with the Holy Spirit without delay. Like all intimate relationships, we must attend to it or it does not flourish. If we ignore our partner then our relationship does not become the great source of nourishment that it can become when we invest ourselves in it and fully participate. To have a profoundly successful relationship we must become devoted.

We demonstrate our devotion through our prayer, meditation, our lowly listening. And we demonstrate it through remembering that our Beloved is in everyone and everything. Jesus said it so well when he said, "What you do to the least of them you do to me." In remembering that our relationship with our Beloved Partner extends to all life, our opportunity to demonstrate our devotion is always apparent. At first it is challenging and then it becomes the greatest gift of all!

Inside of our relationship with the Higher Holy Spirit Self we discover, as Gerald reminds us, that suffering is optional. Suffering is in our point of view. Working with our Holy Partner we can always shift into a higher perspective and out of the view that produces suffering.

The golden opportunity to awaken is always with us. Gerald tells us that it is the purpose of life itself. We must "seek first the Kingdom" and choose to awaken from the illusion.

As I've said to my students many times, what part of "Seek first the Kingdom and EVERYTHING shall be added unto you," don't you understand?

When we seek the things of this world first, then we are always delaying the EVERYTHING being added. It is our choice. It is YOUR choice, dear reader. Will you delay your awakening or will you choose it now?

Reverend Jennifer Hadley
www.jenniferhadley.com

CHAPTER ONE

Introduction

My daughter told me a joke a minister once told her.

"If you want to make God laugh, tell God about your plans."

I get it. God has plans for me and God will reveal parts of the plan only if I make that connection. It is rare when God reveals the complete plan. Yet, I must be willing to be guided. God knows and is pleased to guide.

This is the job of God's Holy Spirit. This being is to guide me to my fullness in God. This means that I have a life that is fulfilling, joyous, and impactful to a world that needs awakened beings. The Holy One assists me in becoming such a being. I experience miracles and begin living a life that I absolutely love.

Through the direction of God's Holy Spirit I experience creation's gentleness. I learn that the universe is kind. I as well become this kindness.
It would be nice to tell you that this is easy. It can be said to be simple, not easy. Each is to grow faith in Holiness and let this being guide us. It loves each of us so completely that it would never even think to hurt anyone. This being is perfect love and its love for you is complete and perfect.

It is important that we have fun as this is the way of Holiness. This Being makes life enjoyable. No strain or struggle. Life under the direction of Holiness is a divine life. It is one that is treasured.

Each day I spend some time with what are termed Spiritual Practices. I choose those practices that best suit my taste and situations as well as some feeling from my spiritual partner who I call my God, or another name my spiritual belief deems appropriate. This means that this spiritual partner is coming from whatever spiritual or religious system I can understand. The one thing that this writing suggests is that this spiritual partner becomes the director of life and certainly my decision-maker.

In some teachings this is called surrender. No concern because this partner has done it many times, and knows each of us intimately. This partner is gentle, understanding, absolutely loving and beyond anything I have ever experienced. It has already arranged much for me to experience each day based on my decision to choose to deepen this relationship.

Notice that I said that I choose my spiritual practices—and my spiritual partner. Spiritual Practices come from whatever spiritual system you have already chosen. It is important that this be understood. No one needs to change religions. Stay where you are and be open to God. God will find each if that is desired.

I learn to live, move, and have my beingness in God. I am not of this world, but can impact it in a wonderful way when I learn to be in it and not of it. Holiness can teach each this.

At some point each must understand that this partner is an agent of God or can be called God so that each learns that this being can be completely trusted. This Being has been awaiting you and me and treats each with patience and humility. This Being is right now in your mind; in my experience it was submerged underneath what I once called life or my earthly definition of existence. Yet it has always been with me and has spoken to me as long as I can remember. Its' words have been few, but clearly heard. This writer understands that the only other voice in this writing is termed as the ego and it is also jockeying for attention. It has sought to dominate my attention with the seeking of earthly pleasures. Ego direction is not kind. I do learn under proper direction to love this ego as well. Emphasis is on proper direction.

We do not really give up any earthly pleasures, but the other pleasures such as joy, peace, love, compassion, humility and seeking a focus on the spirit become more important. I value the intangibles. Joy for example becomes a staple regardless of what I am facing. The ability to remain joyful strengthens the body and faith. Some vital qualities of life are activated.

Hear that? This Being knows better how each can remain healthy or how to improve health. It is no secret that God and agents of God bring forth more than they are asked. Do not underestimate your need for God and God's desire for you. This each will experience.

Understand that no matter how hard you pray or practice spiritual principles, spiritual growth just happens, and grows, deepens and sustains itself as the power and love comes from within. This power cannot be forced.

Begin Again

The words 'begin again' must become a part of our mindset. Some will make mistakes and must continually begin again. All mistakes are small and as we learn to let them be small, we continue moving forward growing and unfolding. Learn to live within that small space between the future and past. It is a peaceful and joyous space. It is now.

Have you ever been really happy? Many of us have had the experience of good times, yet there are few who have had the true joy of peace. As from this peace true joy arises. Part of it is the meeting of our only true friend and allowing this friend to teach us how to live. Then this becomes a life of purpose and true joy. Touching Holiness causes that joy to be like a ringing sound within. This must be experienced.

Part of the difficulty of having long lasting experiences of peace and joy is that we often live in the erroneous self. Living this way speaks to the fact that my body and my personality are not all that I am. When I call these things myself, I am living within an erroneous self. I am so much more than this! I am an infinite being.

Another difficulty we have is the belief that things of the world make us happy. Admittedly there are many experiences of the world that cause a temporary level of fun and happiness; yet, unless a person has had an experience of allowing spiritual forces to take them to himself/herself, there hasn't been an experience of true joy. A shadow of this can be possibly felt after a church service or some other spiritual experience. This is said to be a shadow because true joy is my nature and becomes apparent, just because. It is continuous. It is true satisfaction. It is an aspect of being.

This book is about our personal development of that sixth sense. It is about building a relationship with something that cannot be truly defined. We are to move beyond our five senses and become dependent upon this sixth sense. Yet many call this the use of intuition. It is intuition and more. Please do not think that this writing is suggesting that you further develop your intuition. Spiritual growth is much more than this. This sixth sense contains so much more that our journey, becomes more fun and enlightening if we develop the relationship to be suggested here.

All my talents and new talents are developed under the direction of Holiness. This being coordinates whatever skills I have and enhances them. I am now living under divine direction.

Actually this is a book about a Being that I knew very little about when I started this writing. Yet my inner guide asked me to write a book about the Holy Spirit. One of the reasons that I knew so little about this Being is because so little has been written about this Being. Actually the information has been under my nose all the time through writing my other books and practicing inner work. There have been many books written about God and many books written about the Son of God. Yet little has been written about that third person in the Christian Trinity. The Holy Spirit is the third person of the Trinity of God the Creator, the Son of God (one of God's creations,) and the Holy Spirit. That Being is God, who was created to assist his children and has all the power of heaven and earth within it.

These love forces are in us all and gives us the ability to express the incredible beauty that we are. Most wonderful child of God please let the Creator love you. It is already instilled mechanisms that are there just for you. Nothing is outside of this Being. In God we share so much. Every aspect of life is on its tiptoes waiting for us to step into this wonderful life that has already been designed for us.

Now I must first believe that this partner has been awaiting me. Secondly, I must believe that this partner spirit is a gift from God and that it is in my best interest to seek it out. Let's just say that this Being is all around me and has been waiting for me. However, I cannot wait for things to get worse. I must get in tune with this being right now. We have no idea how difficult life can be without this partner. Maybe we already do know how difficult life can become.

For periods of time, the process of spiritual growth appears as if you have literally lost your mind. Calm down. You have not lost your mind. Yet, the mind purification process will seem to be that way at times. You are allowing truth to literally take over your thoughts.

The fullness of spiritual growth is its import. It allows a person to enjoy and impact life in ways unimagined. The gracious ways and joy is also pretty attractive. They are infectious. The body and the affairs of the body are considered and come under the care of forces that absolutely understand me better than I understand myself.

You may say that you are not interested. Well, please get interested. You have already been chosen. Ignoring your path is not a good thing. For those of you, who know that you have been chosen, please continue reading. For those of you, who wonder whether you have been chosen, please continue reading. All have been chosen; some actually hear the call and choose to answer it with willingness.

For example it is common for someone to have a design for their life and seek to live that design. Well, listen carefully. Most of us have no idea how much pain and suffering we inflict upon ourselves by thinking that we can map out our lives without the assistance of our creator. Personally, I had to learn to let God be God. I had to learn to let the Holy Spirit tell me what my life is about and teach me how to live. It has literally taken years and this writing may help you and me move more swiftly and peacefully through life. This writing may also help avoid some of the pitfalls of ego thinking.

There are some questions each may want to consider:
1. Can you trust that God's Holy Spirit has good for you and all concerned?
2. Are you ready to live a miracle centered life?
3. Can you learn to trust anything or anyone wholly?
4. Do you believe that God knows what health is?

5. Can you learn to communicate within such that this Being can respond to your most wonderful dreams?

6. Is being a victim acceptable to you or are you ready to be a conqueror?

The Holy Spirit was created to assist you in growing into your fullness in God. The Holy One is your guide through the illusionary world your body lives in. This Being is a gift from God and has wonderful gifts from your maker just for you.

One determinant of God creations is that they are eternal. God's creations are like God. Thus, unless it is eternal like God, God did not create it. In effect nothing that has a physical existence has been created by God. Everything that has a physical existence is temporal.

Everything created by God lasts forever and is unchanging. Soul forces meet this criterion and anything that the five senses interpret does not. However, as one grows all senses join in the proper interpretation of things and 'heaven on earth' is actually experienced more completely. Within this writing we will explore why God's creation is so critical. For what God creates can only bless and do wonderful things. Each of us of course is one of God's creations.

Keep this Simple

Learn to esteem the eternal and you have started down the right path. The body was not created by God under this definition and thus is part of the illusion. You access your true power by becoming more aware of yourself as an eternal-spiritual be-ing. Once done, you will also learn that you can undo the temporary, but you cannot change the eternal. Jesus brought a body back to life because he knew that life is an eternal attribute of every-thing God created and the temporal can be altered. This is part of your power as it is part of the power of everything God created. Become clear about who and what you are—through your creation from God—and learn of your power.

The Holy Spirit cannot really see the planet earth, but looks into the mind to seek to understand what is happening with each. Actually since the Holy Spirit is an agent of God, one can say that God through the Holy One is aware of planet earth. This being is aware of things that pass through your awareness for it lives in your mind.

The Holy Spirit is to help each in the spiritual growth process. Get this: you cannot grow spiritually without this Being. Your job is to allow this Being's assistance in that he/she does not automatically come to you because of freedom of choice. Understanding free will, the Holy One stands waiting for you to shows willingness to gain Her assistance. She has an uncanny way of getting around the blocks one can put up with unwillingness.

This basically is saying that those who think that there is something in their physical world that makes them happy are not thinking correctly. Holiness knows that you have a body that must be considered. Yet, nothing, short of Holiness can make you truly happy. The things that truly make you happy are like God and you, they are intangible. Therefore start with the idea that all you want is peace. Yes, each wants the peace of God.

Tell Holiness of the way you are seeing
situations, circumstances and events.
Ask of how Holiness sees things,

CHAPTER TWO

The Incident at the
Bodhi Tree Bookstore

It was a Saturday afternoon and I was in a magic shop watching a magician perform magic tricks. The marketing technique was for me to watch the trick and then the magician would ask if I wanted to purchase the trick. He would teach me how to perform the trick only after a purchase.

Suddenly my cell phone rings.

"May I speak to Gerald Collins?" the voice said.

"This is Gerald."

"Hello Gerald. This is Elizabeth Morrow and I have a vigil assignment at Agape tomorrow morning that I cannot attend. Are you available to take this vigil for me?" she asked.

"Gladly, but which service is it?" I responded.

"It is the third service. You need to be in the minister's office by 10:30am."

"I will be there."

"Thank you so much," she says.

"You are welcome. Have a good day. Goodbye."

"You do the same. Goodbye."

A vigil assignment is one where a person sits in the back of the church in a meditative state and prays throughout the service. Since the service is nearly two hours in length, holding vigil is equivalent to praying and meditating for two hours without ceasing. Prior to entering the service, the vigil holders and others meet in the ministers' office to pray together. That is another forty minutes or so.

The next day after the vigil assignment, I leave the church with the usual heightened feeling that results from such a lengthy meditation. I pick up some flowers on my way to a recital where my friend Shonda is scheduled to sing. This was my first opportunity to hear her and it was with pleasure to be there and she put on an excellent performance. My feelings of praise for my friend may have also been part of the experience that followed.

After having a snack at the recital, we decided to go to the Bodhi Tree Bookstore, one of the largest spiritual bookstores in Los Angeles.

I was sitting in the store reading a book about the Buddha. Suddenly there was a loud thump in a room behind me. Though I noticed the sound, I just kept reading. My friend, Shonda, who was sitting in front of me, leaned to the side to see what caused the noise.

"Gerald, there is a man lying here behind the bookcase," she said.

A man was lying on the floor on his back and his chin pointed straight up. His head was so convulsed that he was choking, suddenly the choking sound stopped, he stopped breathing and his face turned blue.

Shonda, rushed over to him and tried to straighten his neck to allow air to flow through, he was so big that she couldn't move him at all.

"Rigor mortis could not have set in this quickly," she said.

Since she was a school teacher, I assumed that she was considering mouth to mouth resuscitation.

I went to the front desk to ask for help. "There is a man behind the bookcase over there and he is unconscious. Please call 911." I said.

"We do not have an outside line here. You need to go to the office down the hall," was her response.

Feeling somewhat urgent, I ran down the hall and yelled, "Please call 911, there is a man lying unconscious."

"Calling right now," was the response from the concerned clerk.

I returned to the man on the floor. He was lying still and his face was completely white. There were others who had noticed the incident. When I knelt at his side, he didn't appear to be breathing at all. I first thought about giving him mouth-to-mouth resuscitation, however, I remembered that as a spiritual practitioner, prayer was to be my avenue to take with him.

The Miracle
Something came over me, and my mind went totally blank. Calmly, breathing deeply while looking at his face I seemed to be in a trance. A second later his body relaxed and he started breathing again. He still appeared to be unconscious, but after a few seconds, he opened his eyes and sat up. His face was still absent of color.

"Sir, breathe deeply for a few seconds, you have been unconscious for a few minutes and it may be helpful for you to breathe deeply for a few minutes. Let's take some deep breaths together," I said to the man.

We breathed together for a few minutes. He quickly followed my pace with some deep breathing exercises.

Some other person started asking questions to him about whether he has experienced this before. He just ignored everyone else and followed me with the breathing exercises.

The Calvary Arrives
The paramedics came with a stretcher. "How did you get here so quickly?" I asked.

"We just happened to be right around the corner when the call came in."

I went back to my seat, picked up my book and started reading again because I knew the man was in capable hands. I did minutes later hear him argue with the paramedics.

"I feel fine and do not need to go to the hospital."

Shonda then said "How can you just sit there and read that book as if nothing has happened? There was a demon that inhabited that man for awhile. I am very uncomfortable and must leave here now to calm down."

My first thought was that there is only one power and that there was no such thing as a demon.

I simply said, "One power."

"I must go. I am so uncomfortable about what just happened," she responded.

So we left the Bodhi Tree Bookstore.

Later that evening I remember going to the altar in my room to do my evening meditation. For some reason, I asked about the incident in the bookstore. The spirit within me told me that a healing had been done through me. It specifically told me that I had no power to heal, yet it could heal through me. It then told me that the man would have died had I not been there.

What comes to mind now is the Jesus statement "*I of myself can do nothing. It is the power within me that does the work.*"

There is one power. No one has spiritual power. Some believe that they can direct it. *My preference is to believe that it directs me.* I prefer living a surrendered life where I am under its direction.

While I have never considered myself a healer, I do believe that this incident came to teach me something very simple. After reading about healing, the lesson is now a bit clearer. *Joy and the now focus is reparative.* This means that they heal. The "now focus" is awareness of God.

When I think about this incident, I begin to think about how important it is to have the attitude of being constantly aware of the presence of God. On the days when I meditate more than on other days, it is so clear and I am aware of the presence of God. It is a feeling of peacefulness and centeredness. Specifically, it is a space of being present. Nothing shakes that feeling.

I might have been just as troubled as Shonda was by the incident if not for my vigil assignment earlier that day. Shonda's performance was also a consciousness-raiser for me. I had brought flowers for her and considered her the highlight of the performers. She really embraced the audience with her beautiful voice. Yet, because I was so centered that day, nothing would shake that feeling of "all is well." The practitioner vows require that we *Practice the Presence of God Daily* to stay in that zone. Thinking about this incident this vow is clarified as a worthwhile endeavor.

At my spiritual center many have been trained as practitioners who are like assistant ministers. The full training program is about four years. Practitioner may be likened to the way a lawyer practices law or a doctor practices medicine. Spiritual practitioners practice God activities.

Later, my views of the incident, centered on the thoughts that suddenly exited my mind and the clear nothingness seemed to be the conscious activity. An instant of cessation of all thought with eyes open is considered an act where the heart takes over. An experience of pure love had taken place that day. Again, there is no resistance to life.

I am so grateful to have had some incredible teachers over the years as well as the books that have guided my practice. As my thoughts change, so does my life picture. Family and friends also are wonderfully seen and loved beyond past abilities and this is just one of many personal experiences that I have had.

Since Holiness is at the core of our being, miracles are being shared throughout this writing to demonstrate the power that each of us have. Yes, we also learn how to be a miracle worker.

A Beginning Approach

To start, I must understand that I am an infinite being. Thus, what the Holy Spirit desires to teach me is already present and true. Much of my life has been under the influence of human training which often is the opposite of truth. Human training though unnatural is what most so called good parents give to their children. Human training is unnatural because this book will tell you consistently that you are not human. You are a very powerful spirit with unlimited abilities. Humans are taught limits in almost every way.

The Holy Spirit being fully aware of every aspect of my life and knows how to guide me out of the limited training that I have experienced. This one statement highlights the importance of the Holy Spirit. If I try to teach myself, I will use my past as a requisite for my future and I will experience much difficulty. The Holy Spirit knows the potential difficulties I might experience and He simply teaches me how to avoid them.

The most difficult part of the training is building the understanding that spending significant time in prayer practices is valuable. Jesus said, *"Seek first the kingdom and all things are added"* One is asked to build their lives around their prayer life. This means that I must make prayer and spiritual practices the foundation stone of my life, and then the rest of my life falls in place. Admittedly these practices require trust or I might not be consistent with them.

Holiness gives you a few gifts early in this process to keep you on the right path. When you don't see any results of your work, please do not be dismayed. Just pray, pray, and pray. Read spiritual literature that teaches you of your infinite nature. This is your study.

Finally, practice, what you are reading. If for example something you read tells you that everyone is a spiritual being. Then your job is to practice believing this with the persons that come into your experiences. This does not specifically mean that you tell persons this. It means that you attempt to remember it in the presence of others.

Especially practice with the people who are an influence in your life. Practice with friends and family that irritate you. They are your blessings, because you learn how to rise above the obstacles they present. Practice, practice, and practice some more. You will make many mistakes. Don't be too critical with yourself, just begin again. Learn to let all mistakes go and continue forward.

The following prayer is an example of the type of prayer I use in my approach to Holiness. Use this one or create one for yourself. Most importantly, be open to believing whatever prayer you create. Allow your feelings to arise to pull the prayer within.

Beloved Holy One,
I thank you for teaching me that we are one.

It therefore follows that we have the same objectives. Simply the will of God is my will. Please direct me that I may operate as an agent of thy will. It is more correct to state that it is our will. Direct me such that I have a purpose and mission that allow me to impact this world as you would have me do so.

It is my intention to maintain a conscious contact with you. The purpose of this is to assure my direction by you. Each day I want to grow my love and trust of you such that I never worry. I know that worry is nothing other than a sense of separation. Since separation is a lie and I desire to live in truth, I plan by our continuous contact to live a life of truth.

I cannot imagine anything better than a continuous contact with you. This belies human logic, but allows me the expansion of consciousness that I find so attractive. It also feels so good! I am learning that I am a limitless being of power that lives by grace.

I am so appreciative of you dear one,
Gerald

Feelings behind words are important and cement those words into your consciousness. Do not be concerned if feelings are not always strong about whatever you are praying over. Just be aware that "feelings get the blessing."

This means that the spiritual universe is one of tremendous feeling. You already have some feelings about what you are reading now. Otherwise it may not be something that is acceptable to you. You know when the light bulb goes off; just reading words is not the same as feeling and believing them.

Several subsequent chapters have prayers for your consideration. There is more in the appendix which will give you prayers and practices.

Note that I often use the word "please" in my prayers to Holiness. This is averse to having been trained in affirmative prayer which is often a bold statement of truth. My use of the word "please" is a demonstration of my humble approach to Holiness, as well as an attempt to put my ego aside and recognize I am approaching the most beautiful and powerful presence in the universe. I approach my God this way.

Speak to Holiness.
Tell Holiness of the simplest things you
wish to cleanse your consciousness of.

CHAPTER THREE

Awaken and Know

I recall reading somewhere where it stated that God does not behold inequity. In a way this is saying that God is only aware of what God created. For a period of time this was believed to mean that God cannot see evil. There is truth to this as God does not evaluate or judge. God ignores something that does not exist. Something that may be very real to humans can be totally ignored by God. God is not affected by illusionary matters.

God Knows Only Truth

How is one to judge whether something is good or bad? The answer to this is arrived through another route. God knows. In effect this means that God does not interpret. God just knows truth only and extends truth only. What is being said is that God is absolute. What is limited cannot contain or understand the absolute.

In your human state, your way of seeing is to just interpret what you see. Contrast this to a being that is only able to see reality. This is why God knows. As you begin to see your own divinity you actually become what you believe you see. You become like your creator. You begin to know yourself truly. You know of your own divinity. This is how simple spiritual growth is. Your beliefs are just that powerful. Just understand that you can achieve a state where you know. You absolutely know!

Now what is it that you know? I can learn that I am God's child in whom God is well pleased.

There is a wonderful peace in this knowledge. There is comfort here. There is joy. I rest here comfortably at times. Please consider putting the book down for a moment and resting here with me after reading the following statement:

I am a child of the universe in which the universe is well pleased

The ability to see is enhanced by the love of God. This love has a light contained within it that allows one to see. This light of love is sufficient to maintain and sustain each in all endeavors. God is made manifest in each life that operates this way.

Many of us have heard that mankind is in a dream state. Those who reach the state of enlightenment are those who awakened from the dream. The Holy Spirit has the job of awakening all of us from the dream. As any one of us becomes aware of this condition, we must join the great crusade by assisting others in their individual awakenings. In this way we join with the Holy One in its task. This is one of the purposes of this book. We may not have awakened ourselves, yet it is necessary that we help others to do this. In actuality, when we assist others we assist ourselves.

The reason for this is because all of reality is one. As I help others I am helping myself. It is an illusion that we are separate. God created one spirit, which is sometimes called his son. Nothing is outside this spirit. We are all one. As we willingly assent to becoming a pupil of this Holy being we learn that through helping others we grow.

I consider often the ability to be loving or choose love in all cases when I am interacting with others. I may not do it perfectly in all cases, but Holiness knows of my efforts and assists as I ask for assistance when necessary. I as all can learn and improve daily in this ability to choose love.

We are all Interdependent, not Separate

Some years ago I recall listening to a tape of a sermon given by Martin Luther King. In this sermon he spoke about the fact that one cannot get to work in the morning without first using something given us by others around the world. For example, he mentioned that the alarm clock that awakened us in the morning was provided by the Japanese worker, the coffee by a South American worker, a rice cereal given by an Asian worker, and soap by an African worker. This is just another way of saying how we have become so dependent upon one another. This dependence is growing with such creations as the Internet and more of us become multilingual enabling greater communication ability across the planet.

Now this sermon delivered by Martin Luther King was in 1967. He probably wouldn't be surprised to find that our dependence upon one another has become greater. This is a simple example of our growing dependence in the physical world. It is only an example you either accept or not.

Incredible power is available to those who awaken—AND ask. Actually, this power is already available to each of us. For example, Jesus had incredible power before his awakening. He just learned how to use it upon awakening. As one begins the process of awakening, they grow in spiritual strength on their path. It is like saying that you get stronger as you move in the direction of awakening. As you awaken you become a real life.

Many have said that the purpose of life is to learn to love. This writing is saying the same thing in another way. The purpose of life is to awaken. As you awaken your ability to love grows. Thus one might say that this writing is to assist in your ability to love through the process of awakening.

Everyone has this purpose. Take your place among us. You hit a grove that has already been mapped out for you.

Learn to have confidence in your fellows on the planet. In this way you grow your own faith. What is faith, but confidence. Did I say we are one? Quietly have faith in all and your faith grows. This is Holiness. We are one whole.

Religions or Thought Systems
Let's deal with this concept of being a religious person versus being on a path of spiritual growth. Religions are thought systems. Unfortunately many religions get their followers to be too rigid about some things. Many times the things that they get too rigid about are such things as being good or doing things right according to their doctrines. Some of these doctrines have erroneous thoughts within them. Some of these systems pass erroneous thoughts from generation to generation. As a being of unlimited power, doctrines that place rules upon you at some point become hindrances. They really are not wrong. Doctrines have purposes for religious groups. Often they attempt to keep followers in check.

These persons can and do love God as best they can. Erroneous thoughts are just that. They are erroneous. Knowing that it is not my place to judge anyone, it is my place to just let Holiness do what it does with everyone. There will be opportunities to see that each of us is developing a capacity to love. Holiness always meets each of us where we are and can take us further if we are willing.

Being on a spiritual path is a little different. This writer believes that we on a path to just know fully who we are — our Holy-connected Self. I know that I am a spirit made of God's love. This is me at my core. Yet until I operate as if I am truly closer to that 100% of the time, I am just stating it. Until I assume that position of power and grace where I know this fully, I have not fully awakened. However, it is progress to at least know that this is the goal. Isn't this a simple goal?

There is really nothing wrong with being religious; however, this writer is simply stating that a religion is just a start. Being spiritual is also just a start. To actually fall deeply in love with God and be willing to be taught by God is what the author believes is a higher path. The religion then becomes God. Since love was created to be shared, then the lover of God becomes a teacher of God by his/her actions. Yes, one teaches the love of God and expresses this in their way of living.

God or the Holy One becomes the guide and one is not so attached to any written document or doctrine. God is then leading one to where they are most beneficial and can bring the appropriate change that moves our world forward.

It is being said that to know something is good; however, until one operates as if they know, they are still in the partial belief stage. They do not fully know. On the other hand, let's not let the illusion fool us. That is, do not judge your circumstances to determine your level of spiritual growth. If you desire to judge yourself in this way, look at your actions. Your actions tell your more about yourself than what you think you know. Be careful not to critique yourself. Prime thinking is to remember that which you are is already true.

Such actions as being a giver, having compassion, being patient, and living in peace are more accurate determinants of your level of spiritual growth.

These are actions worthy of your seeking and attention. They are more accurate determinants of your growth than what you own or the circumstances of what is termed "your life."

What is Life, Anyway?

Speaking of life, it is also important that we define more clearly what life is. Life is God. Therefore life is good and eternal. The circumstances of your life are just that—the circumstances of your life. These circumstances are such things as your credit score, your assets, your debt level, and the number of people you consider to be your friend among a host of other things. These circumstances are temporal. This writing suggests that learning to live is learning about who you are. The Holy One is the primary being to help you in this task.

The Holy One vs. Ego

This writing will later define the Holy One, give examples of its way of working, and suggest ways of working with it. I once read that if one does this right it will be the easiest thing ever done. This is because your ego, which is usually the only stumbling block, is powerless in the face of what God created. We will later define the ego and provide suggestions on how to deal with it as well. The Holy Spirit is the focus of this writing.

But, why study the Holy One? Well, this agent of God is your true companion in this world. This being helps one to think properly which this writing defines as the purification process. This being will also help one understand who they are and why they are here. It does this in gracious and lovely ways. Your job is to just allow this being to come into your life and become your teacher and friend.

One thing about knowing is important. It has been my experience that thinking that I know impedes my spiritual growth. In order to fully embrace my growth, it has been necessary at times to just let the Holy One be in charge.

Otherwise, my ego is given preference and I can wander off the path.

The Holy One is also your teacher. One of the purposes given to me is to teach. *This requires that I remain a good pupil.* My teacher is the Holy One as opposed to my experiences. It is important that this be understood. My experiences come from my past and the past is a poor teacher. Humanly, we are often taught that experience is a good teacher. The opposite is being stated here. Most of us grew up believing that we live in bodies and spirits are in a spirit world. Well, this spirit, which I am calling the Holy One is in the higher part of our mind and wants each to learn more about himself/herself. To learn what is already true is to just open you to yourself.

So let me redefine growth. Spiritual maturity is humbly letting the Holy One teach you. Didn't I say this a few paragraphs ago in another manner? Your past of human training was not sufficient. Learn to be humble before Holiness!

It is not sufficient to say that we need more God. I must learn to give more to God. Give the problems to God. Turn life over to God. God know nothing about sacrifice. You give up nothing and gain so much more. Turn all the nothing over to God!

The Holy One is also your teacher. Unlike worldly ways of learning, it is necessary that we introduce ourselves to Holiness and become available as a pupil. In this way we learn its lessons and learn about ourselves.

If I operate as an ego, this can be a painful and stressful process. For this reason these definitions must be understood. The ego of you will suffer dearly through spiritual growth unless you place this being in its proper place, you will then suffer along with it. The ego is not to lead your spiritual growth process. It leads nowhere and that will eventually be suffering. Of course, this is not what you want. There has been enough suffering on this planet. At least that appears to be the case.

A person I have a great deal of respect for teaches that suffering is necessary and valuable. Well, I cannot honestly disagree. Yet, I have learned that it is optional. *Yes, suffering is optional.* You will at times experience things that you do not desire. Your job at that time is to recognize where you are. This "where" is a unique question. Are you in your ego or your spirit? Choose to leave that ego existence by correct definition of what you are. When I lived in my ego seeking spiritual growth I suffered. Actually if you are interested in spiritual growth, then live in your spirit. Otherwise you have a prescription for intense suffering.

Live in your spirit by recognition of the earthly existence as one to be forgiven. The body and its affairs will be well and good if you seek to be guided by a loving spiritual being. This is the Holy Spirit. I keep things simple. You can call many things spiritual. Yet the recognition of everything as being composed of spirit spiritualizes your existence. Guidance follows. That guidance and the process of being directed in your forgiveness work are done by this being.

If there is suffering...
At those times of mental anguish, one is usually too engrossed in the world of form, seek to dive into your spirit and ask the Holy One to help you do this if necessary. Be still and be alert to notice what it does for you at that time. Pain should subside if you are willing for it to do so. You may not get it as you desire. However, a choice will be given you to exit pain and suffering. Then you choose. You may decide to call someone and request a prayer. At times of suffering it is often difficult to make good decisions. Just be aware of this. There is a point where pain can become impossible. You want to learn more about this.

To be honest, anyone who lives based upon what he or she sees is asking for trouble. You are on a good path if you are just joyous. The Holy Spirit has an ability to just make you happy. It is from this place of joy that the outer begins to conform. Yet, learn to let this being teach you how to be joyous. There will be times when you are happy without knowing why. Then you will know that you are on your path. Then you will know that you have found your teacher.

One Will

Following is an excerpt from a book written many years ago called *The Pathway of Roses*[12]. It is taken from a chapter entitled 'The Way to Freedom.'

> *There is one will in the universe just as there is one mind. The one mind is the mind of God; the one will is the will of God. The mind of individual man is an individual or differentiated expression of the Infinite mind, and the largeness of the human mind depends upon how much of the one mind man may decide to appropriate. Man has the freedom to incorporate as much of the infinite mind as he may desire, as the mind*

of the infinite is limitless, the mind of man may continue to become larger and larger without end.

The will of the individual mind is a partial expression of the will of God, just as the force of growth that is in each branch is a part of the same force that is in the vine, and the power of the individual will depend upon how perfectly the individual mind works in harmony with the infinite mind.

Without attempting to understand what "one will" means let's just understand that since there is only one life and one mind, that life and mind has one will? To the extent that anyone believes that they have a separate set of thoughts they are in separation. We must learn to release our separate thoughts and let the one will take us where it desires.

This is another way of looking at surrender. Surrender your little life to the whole. Then you must experience life as it has been designed by God. Surrender simply means to let Holiness take over and place you in the divine design.

But, why be interested in spiritual growth? It is the only way to really enjoy life and find a life purpose. Unless the Holy One has told you of your purpose, be careful. This being is your guide provided by God and is the only one that can truly be trusted with this task.

It is necessary to become clear about what a purpose is. Many think that living an abundant life is a result of living one's purpose. Your purpose has nothing to do with having more things. Let Holiness tell you of your purpose. You will live comfortably and absolutely enjoy life. Please be careful about that "wanting" mind. Both Jesus and Buddha spoke about proper thinking. There is much that you can learn from this writing.

Hear this again. You cannot reach a spiritual growth goal without the Holy One. Use another name for this being if your desire. This is possibly why so few get there. Many of us are too busy in the world of effects or we rely on human teachers to help us to grow. Our human teachers do make wonderful contributions. These are being brought to us by Holiness. Nothing is as precise as the Holy One. It does not fail if asked. Ask for its assistance.

Build this relationship and find that it is the only relationship that you need.

It is within the feeling nature that knowledge is complete. Yes, your heart already knows. Keep this vessel open to the Holy One as it is within this vessel the Holy One resides. Our minds are not necessary to knowledge as this is already within the heart. Use the mind through maintaining awareness of what is passing through. The mind does strengthen and clarity is a beautiful thing.

Knowledge is of the heart. Of course this writer is speaking as if the heart is part of your mind. And that is what this writing is premised upon.

Make speaking, writing (possibly in journals), singing and praying to Holiness part of your daily routine. Give Holiness an opportunity to intercede in situations for you. Talk to Holiness. She listens. She responds.

Don't Be Afraid of Love

However, you must not be afraid of love. Do not be afraid of your feelings. Feelings are not always accurate. Stay with the Holy One! Only this being can direct you to understand that you cannot totally trust your intuitive feelings. Unless you are well developed, just speak with Holiness each day and be willing to be guided. Speaking with Holiness is also achieved by entering the silence several times each day. Some times that state is reached in two minutes. Do not judge what that state feels like or looks like. Just start your prayer work consistently. Without words you will then be guided. You do not need to "talk" in this form of communication. You meditate in the silence and the silence, wherein Holiness lives, speaks or just works to reprogram your thinking.

Blindness

In actuality, most humans are blind. They think that their eyes see. They then begin to believe what they have seen or experienced in some way. For example, it is my understanding that everything is composed of God. Now if someone is acting in a way that displeases me and I judge them as not having an ounce of God within them, I have judged incorrectly and left my station of standing in truth. I must begin again.

Beloved, learn of the way that God knows and begin to agree with God. Otherwise, it is again, a prescription for pain. For those on any life path, judgment brings pain. Learn to ask the Holy One such things as "Where am I in judgment?" and let all your pains and inadequacies go. You then learn of the incredibly powerful being you have within you and become what God already knows about you.

The Old Holy Ghost

Some have visited churches where persons have claimed to have the Holy Ghost within them. At times like this, these persons may appear to other like they have lost their minds. As a young child I was suspicious of such persons. Were they just happy beyond understanding or were they just out of their minds? In these churches there are often other men or women who have the job of restraining the Holy- Ghost-infected ones. The speaker (or minister) then has to either delay his sermon or work around all the mayhem. It really seemed like to me that the speaker was successful when there were some Holy-Ghost-inhabited congregants.

Now, though still suspicious of such proceedings, I do understand that the Holy One is the place of extreme joy. It is its job to inspire joy. Through this joy, one can rise above all else in existence to continue the work they must do. This means that the Holy One inspires this joy daily. How would you like a daily dose of joy? The Holy One also inspires a peace that is beyond understanding. Its primary method of operation is this extreme peace that the world cannot give. This is the peace that "passeth human understanding."[11] That peace is beyond this world. It is an inner peace that one simply 'allows' to make their day. Hopefully all days are given to this peace.

The Holy Spirit is literally in the higher part of your mind. Above the earthly thoughts and above the mundane is this part of your mind where this being dwells. Some call this the upper room — the thoughts of God are here, a direct link to the mind of God. Scripture refers to it as the mind of Christ within. Wouldn't you like to learn to think like God? It is through this link that you and I can learn that Holiness is everywhere. It is through this link you learn that anything is possible.

Through the link with the Holy One, we are all literally joined as one. Through our awareness of it, we learn that there is nothing that is impossible to us. This writing is not to suggest that anyone has any spiritual power that is absent in anyone else. One of the purposes of this writing is to help you learn that you have it. Some choose to believe that this power can be directed. That may be answered within this writing.

Believing is Seeing

There is an old world adage that says: "Seeing is believing." That must be turned around to understand what you are asked to do here. God is real. God is reality. You may never see God in its essence; however you do want to enjoy this presence. There is no greater joy than experiences with God.

In order to fully enjoy God, you must heighten your belief that you are always in the presence of God. Then the experiences of God will increase and you will "see" God. That seeing will not be with the body's eyes, but may come in visions or whatever way you are more open to the experience. The critical point is to practice being in the presence of God.

It is being asked here that you increase your belief that you are always in the presence of God. If willing to believe this, what can one expect other than to increase their experience of God? That experience is an abundance of all good. Who wouldn't want this?

Consider the following example: Suppose you spent considerable time among thieves. You would tend to be less trusting of people around you if had such an experience. You might tend to believe that most people you meet are thieves and cannot be trusted. In fact, if you had such an experience of having spent considerable time among thieves, it would be more likely that you would become one. This is because you might believe that this is a "normal" way of living. This simple example is saying that everyone has a mind within that is so powerful that it causes one to experience more of what they believe.

Now turn the attention back to God. You can increase the experience of God in your life by simply being willing to believe that you are always in the presence of God. This is commonly called "Practicing the Presence of God."

It is necessary that we take in some qualities of God that augment your practice. It is necessary to believe that God in incredibly good. It is necessary to believe that God is incredibly peaceful. It is necessary to believe that God is incredibly loving, gentle, and caring. Believe these wonderful things about God and know that God can be trusted as God can only give. God never takes anything away that is good for you.

Be careful of the old beliefs about a God that "test" you with trials. Also be aware of the old spiritual beliefs about sacrifice and the like. God does not ask for any type of sacrifice on your part. God does want to change your belief system. Be careful of giving God qualities of a human parent where such words as "tough love" come into play. God is not human and God can never take on human "issues." God does not know how to be mean nor does God know how to be anything other than loving.

Similar to God's creation of the Christ and the Holy Spirit, God only pours God's total love into its creations. That is why you can call Christ God and the Holy Spirit God. It is because each is fully God. The total love of God was given to each of these beings. This is also why you will perform miracles and grow with the work this book is seeking to teach.

You have all that God has to give already within. The Holy Spirit wants to teach you this so that you will understand it and experience the wonders of such a belief system.

The eyes and the circumstances of life will not teach this. For example, I was once having the experience of poverty. In order to grow out of that condition I had to remember "who and whose I was" as much as possible. I am a child of the infinite one. This means that I am God's child endowed with the power that my parent gave me. That is the power of my parent's love. It is all power.

My poverty circumstances were trying to tell me something different. Such circumstances would not support the belief that I and my creator are one. The lesson here is that you do not use your circumstances to tell you anything. In scripture it says something about lies and father of more lies. This is what your circumstances often do. Your eyes and other senses do the same thing. They do not tell you of the spiritual universe, they thus lie to you. Without appropriate practices and prayers mentioned herein, the five senses may even cause one to judge (perish the thought).

Alternatively, I could have tried to work harder or use a hosts of other things in an attempt improve my circumstances. There were times when I did try to work harder on some things. As a believer in the power of the mind, I found it necessary to focus more on my practices of truth.

Until your mind is changed and you return to knowing more about the true self that you are, just trust that you have incredible parentage (God) that loves without cause or change. No matter what you have done or will ever do, your parentage will not change its attitude about you. Release all guilt. God only loves!

Practices of Value
Ask the Holy Spirit to help you with practices that assist you in believing that love surrounds you each and every moment. Important to understand that this is primarily what the Holy One wants to teach you. It wants to help you to be clear about the power that you are. Its primary desire is that you be willing to believe things similar to the preceding paragraphs. Your willingness to believe such things is the primary need the Holy One has of you. Holy

One will ask little of you. It will ask nothing other than your willingness to believe.

Focus on this term willingness for a moment. If these beliefs are contrary to your past beliefs, this change can seem a lot. Personally, I began to privately practice telling myself that I am God. There is a part of the mind (possibly ego) that will refuse to believe such things. With willingness the Holy One will make sure you have ample opportunities to practice and will help tremendously. A prayer such as the following should help:

Holy One,
My request of you is that you assist me in believing beautiful truths about myself. I am willing to believe these things. I am aware that the value of such beliefs supports me and many others.

I do quite often feel my love for you and our life. These feelings are incredibly strong. I am not afraid of them. Let us grow them together as well.
Gerald

The phrase "Practicing the Presence of God" is common in many circles. In order to do this one must walk through one's day remembering to practice the belief that love surrounds everything. Love is another name for God in my mind. Be willing to let each moment be sufficient for you. With each breath just remember that you are surrounded by a beautiful love, a beautiful peace, and a beautiful joy.

Each thought has an energy signature. Some of these signatures are like clouds that block the light of love. By doing the work of getting rid of some "issues" the clouds pass. I am willing to release the sometimes called negative energy that has become my clouds. Often they come from my past. It doesn't really matter whether my past was good or bad. It is impossible to find all of my issues, but I can clear many with spiritual processes. I might even learn to do nothing and find the grace of that inactivity (perish the thought).

One may choose to just focus on peace alone. As from a peaceful mind, God is remembered. A peace-filled mind is really a beautiful mind. My belief is that peace is the primary quality of a heavenly state.

Peace. Ahh. Peace. Ahh. All is well. This feeling of groundedness is of value.

You may have heard the phrase "The Peace of God." Everyone enjoys the feelings and experience of this peace. Whether you have heard of it or not, consider desiring the Peace of God. Pray for it as an experience. Recall Jesus was often referred to in Scripture as the "Prince of Peace."

CHAPTER FOUR

Leila

I remember very clearly the last morning that Tiger, our pit bull spent with us. I woke up crying loudly. Since my door was closed I assumed no one heard me. I just could not hold back the tears. The entire household had been stunned by the news of Tiger's illness. He had cancer. I guess my tears were because I believed this might be the day he would be put to sleep.

I stopped crying when I heard Tiger lapping water from his water dish in the kitchen. He was so loud that I left my room to go see about him. I opened the back door and walked into the back yard with him. It was painful watching him poop because he was in so much pain.

Tiger was put out of his misery that evening. He had suffered long enough and it was time for him to return peacefully to his maker. Though the entire household loved him, putting him to sleep was our act of compassion. Tiger was only eight years old.

Our other dog, Caesar moaned incessantly looking for Tiger. We tried our best to have someone stay with Caesar every day, which was nearly impossible because we all had things to do.

Caesar started getting out of the yard and running around the neighborhood. Some of our neighbors tried to catch him because he was a very valuable dog. Yet Caesar was too quick for anyone to catch him. However when he saw one of us, he'd lie on his back and wait for one of us to pick him up and carry him home.

Caesar's moaning continued every day. Though Tiger was a pit bull and much bigger than Caesar, they were perfect friends. Caesar joined our household as a puppy a few months earlier, and Tiger was very protective of him

The Birth of the Puppies
One morning three dogs appeared in our front yard. My daughter picked up one of them and took her into the house. She was weak, frail, and hungry. She was a young puppy and immediately enjoyed playing with Caesar. We named her Leila. Soon the two puppies were playing and wrestling throughout the house. Then they would run across the wood floor to the couch making the drum roll sound as their eight paws hit the floor. Caesar's loneliness and suffering came to an end. My daughter cut some of the hair from Leila's face, so we could see the eyes of a beautiful puppy. As she grew stronger, their playing turned to romance and we noticed that Leila began to gain weight, it was easy to surmise that this puppy would soon have puppies of her own.

The puppies were born late one Sunday night. Eight days later the seven puppies have doubled in size and are snuggling up to their mother to eat. The gentle and loving way that Leila came to their blanket and laid down so that the little ones can get to her nipples was so touching. The puppies couldn't see yet, and Leila licked and attends to them with so much love. She seems to know exactly what to do for her young ones. These instincts are natural and support life.

Accessing our instinctual self

This sixth sense is the instinct that all humans have, although many seem not to have it. We read and study incessantly about matters that are instinctual. Watching Leila care for her puppies without any instruction reminds me of this instinct that each of us has. What is it within the human organism that makes it so difficult to access instinct? Is it our inability to stop thinking intellectually that keeps the innate instinct from coming forward?

Many of us have the unnatural habit of not using this instinct that allows us to be in constant communication with our creator. This communication is sometimes called prayer. Yet, since God is our source for everything, shouldn't there be another word for our ability to remain in continuous communication? Prayer has the connotation of our asking for something. My preference is to call this communication, communion. *Communion is the form of prayer where the person intends to lay down their own thoughts and allow the thoughts of God to come to them. It is a deliberate act of humility.*

The ego puts up a defense to keep one from accessing the God presence within. For example, one of the common defenses is the belief that you must work on a problem directly. By spending your time working on problems, one could possibly spend less time focusing on spiritual matters. Jesus made the statement "seek the Kingdom and all will be added." I interpret this as spending time and focus on your spiritual growth and this focus will take your problems away.

In effect, by giving focus to error one may grow the error. Your attention is very powerful. Consider calling all the things you would like to improve about yourself an opportunity. This is much greater than just seeking to be positive. Attention energizes that which is given focus. Be conscious in how you "name things." All things do work together for good. Never give in to regrets or mistakes. Everything has assisted in bringing me to being conscious of this very delicious moment.

Understand the ego's defenses come in many forms so one must use *awareness* to recognize it for what it is. In my ego mind I may see these defenses as something coming from somewhere else and by being unaware; I begin to work on them. Working on them is a waste of time as they simply reproduce themselves. As you work on a problem it may seem real to you. Learn to tell Holiness trustingly about situations and watch what happens. This will tell you of the power available to you.

All blockages to the instinctual sense are mental; believing in what we see keeps us from accessing the truth. Pride, incorrect knowledge, anger, and other mental feelings can be called judgments that can block the awareness of the presence of love. Sometimes I take the time to seek to understand my own motives for an action.

As all minds are one, we have the potential to become aware of anything. This means that we have the potential to be psychic. This psychic ability allows us to be aware of whatever anyone is thinking in the world.

Many of us have heard the story about the wife who is standing beside a car while her husband is under the car working on it. Suddenly the jack slips and the husband is trapped under the car. Without thinking, the wife suddenly picks up the car with one hand and uses the other hand to drag her husband from under the car. She does this without thinking and somehow finds the incredible strength within her.

The wife in the above story suffers broken ribs as a result of lifting the car, but she has saved the life of her husband. This story is the result of not thinking and reacting to a situation, thus this act without thinking has potential beyond just the mental.

Let me now re-introduce the star of this book. This Being is a part of us and has been with us all our life, and loves all beyond one's own understanding. God created this Being to be our teacher and to watch over us eternally. This Being is called the Holy Spirit.

The Power of the Holy Spirit is Yours
The Holy Spirit has all power on earth and heaven. For this reason I can call it God. It really doesn't

matter. I simplify my spirituality by speaking to the Holy One.

One day she was speaking to me and the voice seemed a little different.

"What shall I call you," I asked.

"Just call," was the response.

I assume this suggestion was that I stay in touch.

Begin to see yourself as God created you. God created you in the image and likeness of God. God created you out of God's perfect love. God created you out of itself. You are therefore nothing but perfect love. You are a wondrous and incredible spirit. To be more specific, you are a state of awareness. You are mind within a great mind that is like a merger that must be made. I suggest that there never was a separation.

Seeing yourself as anything else diminishes your true power. Call yourself a body and you separate yourself from your creator. You also separate yourself from what you are. It is like saying that all you can see is not to be trusted. In a way, this is true. Yet, this attachment to a body causes such limitation because the body tells you that this is your reality.

For example, your parents named you when you were born. Over the years you developed a personality and belief about yourself. Now guess what? Much of what you have developed is a lie. You are not a human body. You are only what God created. That is something magnificent. Becoming aware of this magnificence, your personality actually is then enhanced.

As a God creation, you are much more than a body. The body is often ego driven. Your five senses have been programmed by the ego. Now with the help of Holiness, you are to go through a reprogramming, as you become what God created you to be. You are to awaken from that long list of erroneous thoughts that you have grown over lifetimes.

If you have read a bit of history, you are to awaken from many lifetimes of erroneous thoughts. You will get help in doing this from many sources. This is what each of us will eventually do, as we awaken.

Why are we so often told that we can do anything that we believe that we can do? Let's take the "do" out of this and simply say there are unlimited abilities available to us if we can begin to believe it. Begin to see yourself as God's perfect creation and you start down the correct road. It begins with belief. Admittedly these changes do not happen overnight. However, with perseverance, they do occur. It can happen in an instant if one is open to learn.

There are people who use positive affirmations to change their lives. It is possible to repeat something so often that you begin to believe it. Yet, because of prior conditioning this can be a long and slow process. This prior conditioning is constantly being confirmed by what your eyes tell you. You can learn to release yourself to God to claim your inheritance. With the Holy One as your guide, you cannot fail. Beliefs are in mind, your heart already knows. Say to the heart: "Make the choice for Holiness."

Consider the following:

- God gave me the Holy Spirit to help me on this journey.
- All of this power is mine as I begin to let the Holy One teach me.
- Of myself, I can do nothing. Yet, with the Holy One anything is possible.
- I can begin to say such things as "into thine hands I commit my spirit," or "into thine hands I commit my life."

This perseverance must also be tempered with humility. This is because the Holy One sees you as its equal although she knows that you do not know it. She will not force herself upon you because she loves you so and knows of your power *because your power is the same.* Please catch this little assumption. Through erroneous beliefs, you use your power to block the full assistance of the Holy One. This is because in believing something, you are using the power of the mind, which is the same power the Holy One uses. However, erroneous beliefs limit you as they limit everyone.

God's Will

It may seem that we are coming under tutelage or slavery. This is the kind of slavery you want. For some reason freedom becomes greater when this type of slavery is understood. It is a God granted freedom to roam as you desire however you do so with the understanding that this freedom is within God's will. For God's Will is always good and desirable.

Are you able to say, without exactly knowing God's Will, that you are willing to let God's will be done? This is the single Will that is in concert with yours and all. It is a statement of faith. It is a statement of trust in the work of Love. It is your most powerful prayer and a letting of Holiness to provide through your thoughts an avenue for all of us to be consistently ourselves.

Oneness with all there is
There is another condition that you must meet as you grow into awesome being that God created you to be. This is the understanding of oneness. God created all of his children out of the same love. You are therefore not to look at what your eyes tell you to grow in this manner. Conceive of all of God's children as one and you have started down the correct path. Conceive of all of reality as one and you get a better picture. Separate anyone or

anything from this wholeness and you start an attempt to split the mind of God again and return to separation thinking. Begin to think along these lines: "All that there is, is God."

By the way, if you begin to think this way, guess who benefits? You do. See yourself properly and get interested and you suddenly begin to become healthier. Certainly this has been the experience of this writer. You are not to look for benefits. A prayer practice and living in truth has the affect of allowing Spirit to care for you without consciously working in a particular area. Understand that truth is naturally abundant. No strain or struggle. Grace is always available.

Pray for the understanding that you learn the Holy One's lessons of forgiveness. Is it becoming clear why Jesus spoke of forgiveness so often? The deeper spiritual meaning of forgiveness is to be aware of the lies that our five senses tell us. Now you are closer to truth. Learn to "forgive" what your eyes tell you. We cannot fully grasp the meaning of forgiveness with our minds. We let the Holy One teach of these meanings as we remain willing to learn.

It may surprise you that when you look at a situation and call forth Holiness, right before your eyes, those conditions change. Situations will occur to give you practice on calling on Holiness. You begin to see wholeness or Holiness everywhere, and your inner vision improves. As you practice calling on Holiness, the Holy One has no reason to deny you. This is the literal meaning of healing. You can heal because the power of God is yours. God does not withhold, when we are willing to believe.

Seeing is a process of activating observation. Certainly there is some impact upon what is seen and experienced based upon "where" you are in consciousness. Consciousness expands and never shrinks.

Discerning the inner "voices"

As the author of this writing, the Holy Spirit is called the voice for God. This is because it is my way of talking to this Being. It is the voice for God within you as well. You may call it whatever you choose. The Holy Spirit has no ego and is always humble. This voice is your link with God within. There is a reason why this writing uses this link and not a direct path to God. Yet, at this point just understand that within your mind this link is not severable. This is the way that God has no Grand-children as through the Holy Spirit in you God has chosen you, as a child of God, to belong to God.

There is another voice within you. It speaks loudly and often. This is the voice of the ego. This term ego will be discussed in a later chapter. It is a voice you made. God planted the Holy Spirit within you so that you could hear God's voice and choose to listen to this voice. Once you learn to hear this voice you then learn that this is the only one you want to hear. We are now at that place where Jesus says that you cannot serve God and mammon.[1] These are two masters. You choose to serve one or the other. *You cannot serve both.* If you are so stuck in the world guided by what your eyes see, you are in service to mammon. You are in service to something God did not create. The choice to serve God is the choice to hear this voice only and be in servitude here. Here your love flows and joy as well. There is no battle of spirit and form. All form is wrapped in spirit. You and God are in the same party. You and God are one. Love, trust, be open and appreciate all aspects of yourself. All forces are at work in your favor.

Holiness

We must take a moment to look at the term Holiness. Some call this wholeness. They are similar, yet in this writing I am using the term as a mark of God. Holiness is a gentle power. It is a peaceful power. Your Holiness is something you were created with. It is beyond understanding. There is nothing your Holiness cannot do. You have it. I have it. Sometimes this term Holiness is a title given to persons of high religious position. *You also have this title.* It was given at creation and not earned with a position. Just learn to let it come out.

Holiness is impersonal and personally beneficial. The zone of Holiness is one that many enter at various times. This writing is seeking those who desire to live in that zone of incredible peace that is lengthy and desirable.

Consider Holiness as:
- The peace that passeth human understanding. A peace not given nor can any worldly existences take it away. From this peace a joy arises, which in combination with peace is blissful.

- The practice of a disciplined stillness that may be learned through devotional practices.
- Intimate yet impersonal. There is focus, but the larger picture is not forgotten.
- Call it energy or a vibration force. These forces are given your approval to bring their cosmic sweep through you and me.
- Holiness is a feminine power, which simply means that it is gracious (masculinity is often referred to as aggressive).

A person committed to a prayerful life may achieve titles. Dancers enter this state due to intense focus. Entertainers and athletes perform feats that can be called truly amazing. Yet, mental attention and physical training brings this out. Are you aware that together we are blazing a path or opening a portal that many mystics have spoken and written about? Consider it as one of the many rooms of the soul. Liken it to a spiritual channel that we are building together.

Please understand we are raising a tide that will lift all ships. As we accept Holiness into the world, everyone will find spiritual growth to be easier. We are opening a channel for Holiness to consume the planet earth. *This is a personal responsibility, yet it is one that benefits all.*

Many scientific studies have proven that we impact each other in wonderful ways by the field of consciousness. Dr. David R. Hawkins, M.D., PhD, a scientist and mystic has written extensively on this phenomenon. Each species has a field. Some call it evolution. We really do not need to be in conscious contact with each other to impact one another. Join the God party of joy!

It is important that you let Holiness teach you to see. Your eyes were not given to you by God, thus they cannot be trusted to help you here. It is outside your thought system that Holiness brings true vision to you. Holiness makes all of us one. Let your brothers teach you that you can love each other as one, and love your brother as yourself as your brother is you. Learn to desire vision. This is your awareness of truth and your salvation. Let not the world and its little trinkets blind you to truth. God is truth.

Out of Time

The voice of Holiness is often out of time. I have awakened some mornings and find that I have the answer to a question I had. I may even hear a voice and not remember when I heard it. Holiness also communicates through dreams and visions while I am either awake or sleep. They have no time element. They just happen and have meaning and purpose. Understand that Holiness lives in eternity. Please understand that our maker does not live in time, nor do we.

A Prayer on Love

This prayer is a simple prayer of remembrance. There is a tremendous feeling of peace that is boundless in the spiritual realm. Of course love is everything and always has been shining like a light that the eye cannot see. Experience this light with joy, bringing true happiness.

> *I pray that I keep in my awareness the tremendous love that God has for me and that it remain in my awareness the love that I have for God.*

There will be or have been times when one feels the powerful attraction of love as our nature that is an example of the "seamless space." This love bridges each with everything in their environment. For this reason an attitude of appreciation, open mindedness, and love is given and received with everything. All things are opportunities to experience this. Consider making your own practices for these thoughts. For today or a few days, everything you see is looked upon with the awareness that God is contained within that thing whether it is animate or inanimate.

Forgiveness

The following forgiveness prayer suggests that the world we live in must be forgiven. Most see the world through an unhealed mind. Consider if one believed that this world was a world of love. Wouldn't one look at the world differently?

Some news stories speak of a great deal of violence and injustices in the world. However, is it possible that this is not true? I do believe that God would not create such a world. The concept that I am suggesting is that each sees a world based upon their belief system. If each believed that the world is a world of love, each would look at the world differently. Further it is suggested that a loving God would not create a world of violence and injustice. God created a world of love is what is often referred to in Scripture as the Kingdom of Heaven. One need not wait until death to experience such a world.

A mind healed by the Holy Spirit experiences a very different world. One might still see news injustices and violence, but it would be viewed differently. A healed mind is one that is not driven by the ego. That mind experiences love through the world of the beholder.

Once your mind believes that love is everywhere, the world loves you in return. Can you believe this? Is it possible that I simply experience what I believe? This is one of the objectives of this book. As your mind heals, your experiences change. Love will love you so sweetly you will find it difficult to believe that there is any other way of really living.

Recall the 91st Psalm in the Bible. In this Psalm it says that a person will see death and destruction, but it will not come "nigh thy dwelling place."

Wouldn't you want this kind of life? This is what happens when your mind is healed. You become impervious to the world of effects. You come under the "shadow of the almighty." A healed mind is naturally protected by the beliefs of that mind. Another simple way of saying this is that there is no ego driving your life. Most of our world lives under a mind that is driven by human training. Much of this is ego training.

Forgiveness Prayer

Beloved One,
It is my desire to have a healed mind. I understand that I can achieve such a mind by forgiving myself for believing what I see in the world. I also understand that I grow to understand that the world is a world of love. I can learn to see the world through eyes of love.

These are the eyes that you have Holy One. Please share them with me. Love is what I am so it is possible that from such a state, I can more completely enjoy my life.

I therefore forgive myself Holy One. I forgive myself for once believing that this world I once saw was all that was in existence. I know that there is more. My creator would not create a world of violence and destruction.

I am willing to believe that my creator created another world for me. I am willing to walk through this world with truth on my mind. Love is truth. I am willing to live in truth. So appreciative of your assistance Holy One,

Gerald

Consider rewriting this prayer in your own words. Otherwise, just consider spending time with it. Contemplate the beauty and power of forgiveness. Accept the power of forgiveness. Accept that your eyes have not been trained to see properly. Forgiveness will give you such eyes.

It is necessary at this point that we discuss the concept of vision. The Holy One may start giving you visions (if they haven't already started). These will be incredible ideas and dreams that may seem weird. They may happen at night while you are seemingly sleeping. In my experience the Holy One gave them to me at many times of the day and night. Most often they happened upon my initial awakening early in the morning. One time I had a most memorable experience while walking down the street in the middle of the day.

As visions begin, ask Holiness how you should interpret them. Be careful about assumptions from an unhealed mind.

You have not lost your mind. A new world is opening up for you to enjoy. Enjoy it.

CHAPTER FIVE

A Ski Trip

I was in Vail Colorado learning to ski. On the first day we were being taught how to ski downhill by swerving laterally from side to side. This meant that one must not go straight down the mountain. One must start out to the left or right, reach a point and then turn and start a diagonal down the mountain to the other side. This looked simple, yet I was having difficulty with it. We were also told that a complete stop was done by turning the skis and planting both skis on edge, digging into the snow which causes a stop.

On the second day I was flying down the mountain out of control. Upon approaching another skier, my skis clipped the skis of this person. As I flew by I noticed that this person fell. Feeling concerned I suddenly planted my skis and came to a complete stop. I then apologized to this person.

I noticed that I completely stopped without thinking, because I was so concerned about hurting him. Up to this incident, I wasn't able to master the stop. I was barreling down the mountain on snow and ice as I was stumbling through a process of learning. Actually the process involves turning the skis until they are parallel to the base of the mountain. Then one is to dig the edges of the skis into the snow. Yes this easier said than done. Yet others were doing it so it must be possible for me.

I did a perfect stop without thinking. What a concept! The cessation of thought, if I can remain in that zone of not thinking I can do anything. This is that "out of time zone" where God and I are one. Yes, God can do anything, and when I get my small thoughts out of God's way, God can do anything through me.

Allow Divinity to Shine

Consider some of my story so far. My thoughts seemed to disappear when I was in front of that man who collapsed at the Bodhi Tree Bookstore. Leila seemed to know exactly what to do to care for her puppies. She was a puppy herself and received no training in their care. I did something instinctive coming to a complete stop on skis. There seems to be something in my mind that can do so much when I get out of my own way. What I have thought to be me is really a block to my real self.

A famous philosopher once made the following statement: "Get your bloated nothingness out of the way of the divine circuits."

Isn't this saying the same thing? You are to learn to let go of your humanness. It is ok to be humane, yet not human. You and I are more than just human. Learn to stop claiming to just be human. We are divine. We are to learn of our divinity. Begin to imagine how powerful you are. When you are willing to let holiness teach you, you can become more that you ever imagined.

Now let's look at this from the viewpoint of truth. I am a state of awareness. As a state of awareness, I am one with my creator. Only my thoughts of being human cause me to be limited. I am therefore limited only by my thoughts. Sit with this a moment and let it sink in. We will come back to it.

God has no grandchildren. This statement means that each of us has direct access to God. We do not need to concern ourselves with our supposedly human lineage. We don't need to believe the teachings that suggest an intermediary.

Re-Interpreting Jesus

The Christian teaching of Jesus as an intermediary must be dealt with here. Jesus made the statement that one cannot get to God except though him[2]. This may have to be interpreted differently. Jesus recognized himself as the son of God. Therefore in order to become God's child, you must become Christ as well. Remember God only has one child. God created one Spirit Being as God's child. You are that Spirit Being as is every person and everything on the planet. Another way of looking at the oneness concept of spiritual science is being given to you again.

God and each of us are one. Doesn't this sound funny? We are talking in spiritual terms. There are approximately six billion humans on planet earth. However, spiritually, God has only one child. All of us humans live through this one child. Actually all of life is one. Christ is part of God. You are therefore part of God. God extended itself to create the Christ (its child) and this belief opens the door to learning other things about you.

Body and Spirit

If each of us is to grow spiritually we must give up the belief that we have a form. We are a spirit and spirit by definition has no form. However, this form has been confused as our identity. The body has purpose and we let that purpose be shown to us. Each human is a perfect and eternal spirit.

Our bodies are wonderful instruments. It is incredible how it sustains itself through the appearance of containing a life. Its' digestive system processes food that we eat and turns that food into muscle, bone, and blood. Its' respiratory system brings air into the lungs. Through the respiratory system, oxygen is separated from the air and sent through the circulatory system to all parts of the body through the blood bringing necessary nutrients to all parts of the body. Yes, the body is incredible.

Unfortunately, the body also experiences pain, suffering, decay and it dies. Yet death and the body are not of God. God had much higher plans when creating a perfect spirit, forever protected by God and living in heaven with God. Do you want to wait to die to experience this heaven when you can experience it now? The Holy One can give you a taste of heaven here on earth. This is done by defining yourself properly and turning yourself over to this teacher, as you begin to experience joy without knowing why. True and long lasting joy is not of this world. You must not even look at the conditions of your situation in order to understand because this joy just is.

In spite of the seeming magnificence of form called body, it pales by comparison to what God has done. God creation is perfect, never changes, eternal, whole, complete and joyous all the time. Clearly many bodies are not whole, perfect, and complete. Recall the conditions (eternal and unchanging) to determine if God created it and you understand that God created things are formless.

Whole Perfect and Complete

Some years ago I was in the prayer ministry of my church. This is a room in the church where we sit and take calls from anyone calling for prayer. What a pleasure to take calls and pray with people from all around the world.

A person called for prayer and asked that I say the prayer after she hangs up. She didn't want to hear the prayer. When asked why she did not want to hear the prayer she took the time to explain it to me.

"Many times when I call the person praying refers to me as perfect, whole, and complete. That irritates me," she says.

"I assume that you do not see yourself as perfect, whole and complete," I say.

"Yes, it irritates me to hear those words. I do feel a bit better after I hang up even though I usually do not hear the prayer," she says.

This incident happens too often as we hear spiritual truths and expect the physical world to exemplify those truths. The important thing is that you do not let the physical world fool you. *You are whole, perfect, and complete in spite of what your eyes tell you.* Every aspect of your life in the outer realm responds to this belief when you hold onto the spiritual truth. You are as God made you. Seek to believe this.

Actually there is a spiritual suggestion that one can "fake it until you make it." Often this means to be positive, even before you fully understand. My suggestion is that you begin a life of prayer and begin to journal what you seek to believe in terms of spiritual truths. It takes effort to hold to new truths especially when they are different from what you have always believed. Please remember that the power of spirit seeks to support your living a life of truth as you move forward.

Many believe, for example, that God created the planet earth. Certainly there was a time when this writer believed that. Some believe that God created a perfect earth and humans messed it up. It is your choice what you choose to believe. In order to awaken you must learn the truths about what God made. Our definition of God creation does not agree with this belief that God created the earth.

Now we can come back to the understanding that God has no grandchildren. Each of us is God's child exactly as God created us. Each of us is a perfect spirit one with our creator. One means that there is no separation between God and the child of God. Spirits do not have separate identities. When God created a child and endowed that child with the power to create, that power was the presence of God itself. God gave us the ability to see the God within us. God gave each of us tremendous power by giving God to us. Thus, all of us being one with God, we can see that God has no grand-children.

One purpose of the writing is assisting the reader in ascending to these truths. Specifically, we are to learn to live the life God created us to live. We were created to create the beautiful, to create the magnificent, to create and live lives of pure joy. By not knowing who we are, we can create unknowingly miserable lives that reject or underestimate the true power and magnificence of our creator. Our problems are more real to ourselves because we are trying to solve these problems on our own. The mind is an extremely powerful instrument. Anything it believes becomes seemingly true. Therefore during this time of transition we must be careful about what we believe. This writer had to begin the process of carefully questioning his belief system. It is common to become overly attached to that which one creates as it seems to be a possession.

In this way we are actually like God. God holds the Christ close and no one or thing can do this child any harm.

Waking Up

God makes no mistakes. In creating another spirit, God limited the creative ability of that spirit. We can make a world that seems to be at war within itself. Yet all of this is part of our collective dream. Each of us is asleep. Not one part of the planet earth is as God would make it. Regardless of which part one is looking at. All that God makes is eternal. For that reason, all that we see was not made by God. This is why when the Buddha was asked about himself, he replied that he had "awakened." Jesus is another of the children of God who awakened. It is understood that Krishna also awakened from the sleep that most of us are in. I assume that there are many others.

In the infinite wisdom of God, some aspects of God are limited in their ability to create. This aspect creates the temporal. That is why this world that we have created is an illusion. That is why our five senses cannot acknowledge the world of spirit and is unable to reveal truth to us. Yet somehow we know that there is a God. Somehow we know something of the spirit world in spite of the fact that we cannot see it.

One can only guess that the many avatars and mystics who have lived on our planet have done us this favor. These wonderful spirits have revealed to us aspects of the world and many truths that God has created for us. It is suggested that this is the reason why these celestial beings had bodies. They wrote or spoke to those separated brothers and sisters to tell them of God and the truth about creation.

The process of spiritual growth is a process of study, prayer, and practice. Specifically, many of us learn some things through meditation. Yet most of us meditate just to open the mind to truths that we later read about.

This writer is seeking to further awaken. One of the purposes of this writing is for the reader to join me in this process of awakening. So come along as we saunter on the wonderful path to awakening. It is a process of becoming aware of our true existence. It is a process of being a creator. It is also a process of learning of the reason for our existence.

Find the reason for your existence and live that reason. One of your reasons for existence is to know thyself. It is by grace each of us lives. It is by grace each of us is fed and clothed. This is how our creator operates. Let the creator love itself through you. It is fun and simple. However, we must eject errors from our minds to do this. We don't need to find our errors specifically. We must just be willing to let go of erroneous beliefs by learning truths.

It is actually possible at times to let go of all beliefs. This is a good meditation topic and a powerful way of living at times. Living and meditating in the now, away from past and accept that God is. Believe this and let the rest occur.

The world that we appear to live in is constantly bombarding us with incorrect information. In order to grow into your magnificence you must constantly remind yourself of truths that you are truly blessed. You begin to learn and accept that Holiness is the only one who can really teach you how to grow. Only God knows the most beneficial route for you. You cannot do it by yourself nor trust yourself with this task. You have been too conditioned by the world to do this.

Another Holy Ghost Story

The ski story was included to bring up an important point. The first point is to begin to control a wandering mind that is always thinking and trying to figure out things. One can stay in the presence of divinity by being present. The second point is that you have been gifted with a spiritual presence that has been with you since your creation. God knows that we are living in an illusory world and has gifted us with the Holy Spirit to help us navigate through this world of illusion. The Holy One is a spirit being God created to help his children who believe they are separate from their spirit.

Here is the story: My aunt told me that she had a job in Chicago where she would leave work at about 6pm, and during the winter months, it was dark. She had to walk across a dark parking lot to get to her car. She was afraid. One evening as she left her job the fearful feeling came over her. Suddenly she heard a voice within say:

"I am with you. Do not worry about anything as you cross this dark parking lot."

My aunt told me that the voice she heard within was the voice of her deceased earthly father. Since she recognized the voice, she let go of the fear and was never afraid of that dark parking lot again.

It wasn't until years later when thinking about the Holy Spirit that this story came to my mind. Though my aunt believed that this was the voice of her earthly father, I believe the voice to be the Holy One using a voice that my aunt would trust. This is the way it works. The Holy One loves you and uses all its knowledge of you to help you.

It is also the job of the Holy Spirit to help rid us of any problems that we believe we have so that we can resume our job of extending creation. This means that the Holy One wakes us up to the understanding that we were created to create, to love and to share.

All power on earth and heaven is within the Holy One and therefore within you. It is through this link with God that you begin the purification process of your mind. Purification is necessary so that your holy mind contains only what you think with God. The process itself is not painful if each of us continues gleefully on this path. Resistance is futile. It is this resistance that creates pain and suffering. *Resistance is of the ego.* We will get to this ego thinking later herein.

Erroneous Beliefs

Up to this point several common erroneous beliefs have been mentioned. The first you may have noticed is that you can't think on your own. My purpose with the ski story is to illustrate that through the cessation of thinking wonderful things occur. Is spontaneity is a way of life? Imagine that God and all the power of God is in you. What inhibits your ability to access that power? *Only your belief that you are separate from your creator causes you to operate as a limited being.* Yes, it is being said here that you have no ability to think on your own

The many avatars and mystics who have walked our planet have sought to teach us these wonderful truths. However erroneous beliefs must be dealt with. Erroneous beliefs limit us and it is the job of Holiness to free us. That is why the truth sets you free. Holiness is truth and extending truth is the job of the Holy One.

I recall a class that I took at my church when a woman walked in and said that she did not believe in God. Though I heard the comment, I chose to ignore it. I also remembered a time when I felt that way. Although most of my life there was a being inside of me that I talked to very often, I just didn't call it God. Now I call this being who has been guiding me all of my life the Holy Spirit.

It is not my place to judge this woman who entered the class. It is being brought up to make a point. You have five senses in your body. These senses will continually try to teach you to believe them only. This is what is called human conditioning. You are not being asked to ignore your five senses. *You are being asked to start down a path toward truth.*

My earthly father was once involved in a religious group that did not support their children going to college. They believed that if you got too much education you will forget that there is a God. I really do not believe that there is anything wrong with becoming more intelligent. However, there are things in our thinking that get in the way. This possibly leads to a way of thinking that does not have your best interest at heart. Later we will define this part as your ego. You do not have a separate mind.

If you choose to believe there is a beautiful, loving, and joyous being within you, allow this being to come out as it is gentle and kind. It also loves you with a love you cannot truly imagine.

Anything you have complete belief in you can do. How about simply raising your left hand right now? Did you have doubt that you could not raise that hand? If you have no doubts, you can do it. That is why confidence is so powerful. Anything you have confidence about you do without fail.

I am thinking about sports athlete, Shaquille O'Neal who makes millions of dollars a year. This particular extremely gifted athlete had no confidence in one area of his game and is such a failure in this area. The owners of the team spent huge sums of money, teaching him how to shoot free throws. Yet he never improved consistently in this area. The reason is his lack of confidence in this area. Surely Shaquille practiced and practiced and practiced. Yet there was little improvement. Fans groaned each time he approached the free throw line.

Think about an area of your life that you are good at. I would bet that you believe in yourself in this area. This same is being asked of you regarding your spiritual growth. Gain confidence as you grow spiritually and you will do it. Another reason that you should have confidence in this area is because God desires that you live in truth. Most definitely these areas may not be tangible. No one is alone in this. God's power becomes available to you when you seek and become aware of your true existence.

It is only your thinking that limits you. Fully aware, the mind is constantly working, most of us have had little experience in slowing down the mind. Such monumental works as *The Power of Now* by Eckhart Tolle is one of the books that I suggest you read. In this book, Eckhart Tolle also provides much information about the ego which is also a lengthy chapter in this writing. There is extraordinary power in staying in the now and somehow slowing the roaming of your mind. In actuality there is no human part of your mind. There is only a human belief.

Another area mentioned earlier is death. No one ever dies. Bodies pass on. Yet, each of us is life. Spirit is life. For this reason it is OK to miss and grieve a person in their human forms as we saw them with our eyes. Yet if you mourn anyone, do not mourn their death. Your mourning can be for other reasons. No one ever dies. Death is part of the illusion. Actually nothing including pets and anything alive ever dies. This understanding should have the benefit of shortening your mourning process and time. You may ask how this writer knows this. Well, I can give you some references that will be other writers. Yet, let me just tell you that there is no doubt within me about this. It has come to me.

And from me this information is being passed to you.

You will gain great benefit from believing this. Those benefits will come to you as you experience death of loved ones in the physical world. Be patient with yourself. Accept truth and allow it to bring you its goodness.

Feelings vs. Love

This is why love is so much fun. The human concept of love is not what is being spoken of here. Yet, even the common human concept of love initially feels good. You see, God is love. Maybe we need to create another term to call love and a separate one for that area where we have feelings for others. Yet that feeling for others is a movement in the direction of love. Please understand that it is just a movement in that direction. *Feelings alone are not love. Certainly the strong attachment that some call love is not the kind of love God has for us.*

With feelings do you feel some kind of a pull? In feelings there is a draw toward a person. This is a hint of what love is. True love is the recognition of the oneness of all life. Do you get this? If love is a pull toward another, it makes sense that this pull spiritually means that we are one. The love feeling is simply a pulling sensation telling us of our oneness.

Guilt

As anyone begins to unload guilt feelings they can then begin to feel the powerful attraction of God. Guilt is somewhat of a block. The powerful attraction of God is stronger when this guilt is not present.

Understand that guilt is something from your past. Let it go. It has no value for you. Please do not accept guilt, nor should you attempt to place it upon anyone.

I have an incredible love for my creator. Each of us does as this is natural. This is true as it was part of my creation. The best that I can do is to give in to it. This is sometimes called surrender. Once again, nothing is lost in this type of surrender. Joy evidences it. Peace evidences it. Perfect peace is perfect health.

Imagine that the grace of spirit is yours.
Allow Holiness to bless you with it's'
goodness. Take your place among us.

CHAPTER SIX

The Three Trinities

There are three trinities that will be explained in this chapter. Trinity means threefold — meaning three distinct beings or parts. Yet, each Trinity will help you understand the Universe.

Author, Ernst Holmes, created a spiritual teaching called the Science of Mind, introduced one trinity. The First Trinity is the mind which is broken up into the conscious mind and the subconscious mind. The third part of the mind is body.

The Second Trinity is the common Christian Trinity of Father, Son and Holy Ghost that is in the Bible.

All three are fully God. This is the second trinity to be explained in this chapter.

The Third Trinity is spirit, mind, and body. This Third Trinity has in it a way of looking at the objective of bringing heaven to earth.

All three trinities have purpose. They are not opposing. Understanding all three can help you tremendously. Each of these trinities deals with the nature of God. That is, each seeks to explain that God has three aspects that operate within the oneness of God. Oneness means that these are not separate parts of God. Only in the physical world do we learn of parts. In the spiritual world we explain things differently; everything is contained within the one. The physical world is contained within the spiritual realm.

One example of this is the ocean. While the waves are part of the ocean it is in no way separate from the ocean. The waves contain all the ingredients that every other part of the ocean has. However the wave is still the ocean. The important point here is to help us understand the world of spirit. In the world of spirit, all things are contained within the one. The spirit world is seamless. Nothing is separate from anything else.

The Science of Mind or New Thought Trinity

This trinity explains the way things take form in the physical world. In order to grow a plant, for example, there is the seed, the soil, and later the plant. In order for a child to be born, there is the father, the mother and later they have a child. Taking this a little deeper there is the semen of the male, the egg of the female, and the embryo that grows into the child. This creation that science has taught us is true, yet so much more has already happened.

In each case there is a threefold process. It takes parts one and two to make part three. The actual process of the Science of Mind teaching is that your mind has three parts.

1. There is the spirit or thought.
2. There is the soul which receives the thought.
3. There is the form that results from the thought being planted within the soul.

Only the third part is visible to the eye. Both the thought and the soul are invisible. Yet each is recognized as part of the mind.

Planting a Lawn

In order to better explain this process lets use the planting of seed with a little more specificity. Suppose you stand on the front porch of your house and look out on the front lawn. There is a sidewalk that divides your lawn into two parts. One is on the left, the other on the right. You decide to replant your front lawn. You therefore rent a tiller and turn over the dirt on both portions of this lawn. You then break up the dirt so that the lawn is smooth and the soil is made of fine particles. This is opposed to having soil that has large chunks of dirt that are hard and make it difficult for the roots to penetrate.

Over this fine dirt you spread some moist fertilized topsoil that is ready to receive seed. You then decide to do a little experiment with this lawn. You decide to spread expensive grass seed only on the left side of the lawn, the seed grows quickly into a lush and beautiful lawn. On the right side nothing is planted.

Each day the entire new lawn is watered. It is helpful to water this grass in the evenings so that the sun does not have an opportunity to heat up the water that is put on the grass. On this left side where the grass seed is planted it is necessary to cut the grass every ten days or so. This helps the grass to grow thicker as the clippings contain more seed. Thus, this left side is growing into a thick, attractive green grass. In order to improve the appearance it is necessary to use an edger to cut a straight line near the sidewalk to improve neatness. It is also necessary to physically pull any weeds that grow on this left side every ten days, so that grass is given opportunity to occupy the soil. All grass seed in spite of the quality have some weed seed. The higher quality grass seeds have less weed seed.

After about eight weeks there is an attractive lawn on the left side. It is one that most homeowners would be proud of. After cutting this lawn and using the edger along the side walk it is a well manicured piece of work.

What is happening with the other side of the lawn? It was prepared just like the left side; the soil was broken up, fertilized, and watered on the first day. However no seed was planted and it was not watered after that first day. What do you supposed this side looks like? It looked like an unkempt lawn full of weeds. Weeds are a result of leaving a field fallow. The soil picks up something because it is the nature of a fertile field to grow something.

Our mind is the same way. It is a fertile field. If you have no life objectives or specific ideas of where you want to go in life you grow weeds. You are influenced by what you watch on television, that which you read in the newspapers or what you talk about with neighbors or co-workers on your job. It is time to be aware of what occupies a great deal of your attention. Preferably much that gets your mental attention is positive.

Notice that the owner of the lawn had to go through the lawn and occasionally pull out weeds. These weeds occupy the same soil that the grass seed would occupy. They also multiply their own kind just like grass does. Therefore we pull these weeds all the way down to their roots to give them little chance of occupying space in the soil. Likewise with things that we do not want in our lives, we can spend time pruning our negative thoughts so that we do not give these things time to occupy our consciousness.

Just breathe through your thoughts or experiences that seem not to be good. The, This Is Perfect, or "TIP" brings awareness of love that allows anyone to turn away from the weeds in this way. Learn to focus on good.

Our emotions are like fertilizer to the things planted. They support growth of all kinds. Your emotions are used to fertilize the beliefs that you have. They bring into existence what you are planting more quickly and with much energy.

Do not be fearful about information. Simple inquisitiveness is fine. Be careful what you allow to become part of your belief system. Mind training is necessary, and willingness to be open to new information is a good thing.

Conscious and Subconscious Mind
Now let's return to our discussion of the trinity.

- There is the conscious mind, which can be called that part of the mind that you think with. You are aware of what is in your conscious mind.
- There is the subconscious, which is called the soul. This is the part of your mind that

can be called the law. It simply executes the orders of your conscious mind.

- There is the body--which your five senses can observe. This is the only part of your mind that the five senses can experience. After your conscious mind plants something into your subconscious it then takes on a form that you can see — it is the body of your affairs, not just your physical body.

In order to understand this further, let's analyze this a little deeper using the lawn example. Many of us have heard the phrase "change your mind, change your life." What you allow to pass through your awareness on a regular basis grows into your life circumstances. In order to make rapid changes it is necessary to keep the mind pliable. You must find the hard places in your mind and break them up like the hard ground of the soil. It is more difficult for new ideas (seeds) to take root if you have hard places in your mind. These are the parts of your mind that are already made up. A made up mind is harder to change. Such as hard headed people who have strong beliefs that are difficult to change.

On the other hand, a made up mind also experiences more stress because it has no desire to change. The outer world is always changing. If one doesn't accept that change is necessary, they are in for a stressful life.

There are some things that you want set in your mind.

1. You want to be firm and unwavering in your mind about the belief that life is good.
2. You want to be firm in your mind about the belief that the universe is a universe of love that supports and loves you.
3. You want to be firm in your mind about the belief that the creations of God and have God within them.
4. Be firm in the understanding that you are not being highly opinionated. There is only one truth that is beyond doubt. That is that the presence of God is everywhere. Lean on truth.

We cannot leave this discussion without dealing with the area of belief. If you believe something, it is true to you. In the Sermon on the Mount, one of Jesus' most famous sermons, he said "It is done unto you as you believe.[3]" Some of the things in your mind that are erroneous seem to be true in spite of the fact that they are false. Our eyes tell us many lies. If you believe something and you have hardened your mind about something, it will seem true. Actually there may be some lies that cause you to appear to have an issue. The feeling of uneasiness that is often felt in the chest area around issues is your spirit trying to tell you that this issue is a lie. Alternatively, it may be your ego trying to tell you that this issue is true. In either case it is the same result. Something is trying to communicate something to you. It may seem to be one of your "triggers." This is one of your choices.

You are so powerful that you create a full set of circumstances and your outer world aligns up to confirm those circumstances when you believe. Be careful about what you choose to believe. Much of my past beliefs were judgments that were erroneous. You can actually live in this world peacefully if you absolve yourself of such judgment. Do not judge. Let the Holy One teach you how to let reality come to you.

Another View of Forgiveness

The outer world is to be forgiven. This is a little different from the worldly definition of forgiveness. I can learn to look past the outer and accept the spiritual truth. This is true forgiveness. Otherwise I live in judgment of the outer and accept the judgment of my previous way of seeing. Unfortunately humans are often taught that having good judgment and learning to analyze things is good. I use this analytical ability less when I just observe without judgment.

My choice is to learn, or be willing to see through the eyes of forgiveness or the eyes of judgment. If I choose to see and only believe through my old eyes I will continue to sin. Yes, it is a sin to believe what the eyes see. You know that there is a God, but your eyes do not see that God. Therefore, when you see something that is not God and believe it, you are sinning. Forgive yourself for believing what your eyes tell you. These eyes were not created to see the truth. They are part of the body and thus only see what the body sees in the physical world. They do not see the spiritual world. Thus they do not see the entire picture.

It has been my experience that there are some things that support my spiritual growth in truth and some things that inhibit it. Personally I have decided not to look at television too often because the television supports the world of illusion. If I am seeking to grow spiritually, which means that I have chosen to listen to my spirit and put less reliance on the tools of spiritual ignorance — the five senses. Hear this: The five senses were made to support the world of illusion. They do not suggest the presence of God or the truths of spirit. This is why the mystics or those who pray and meditate have written books and sought to tell us more of the truths of God.

The Media and Television

The television is seeking to *sell* the illusion. Is this what you want to buy? I am not just speaking of the advertisers. I am speaking of the common thought, and most common thought is erroneous. Simply common thought is not aligned with the harmony of universal forces. Television is a bundle of common thoughts. Very little true learning results from watching television.

While hiking some years ago I heard a teenager tell another child of the dangers of television:

"I read that television is a brainwashing device. This article said that the brain waves are similar to their activity when watching television as that when one is asleep," said Cindy.

"I really don't understand what you are saying," said Rosalind.

"To me it means that I am being given information in my sleep. That is like being hypnotized and something is being suggested to me," Cindy then explained.

"Oh, I see. In that way I can be told to buy something that I don't really need," Rosalind then said.

"Yep, that is what it means," Cindy suggested.

Consider the parts of the mind just discussed. If my conscious mind is not filtering the information coming to me while watching television, it is like being brainwashed. My conscious mind is like a filter. When I relax that mind habitually while watching television, and the television is telling me something, I am more apt to subconsciously believe it. Television is dumping information into my subconscious. Can I trust the networks that much? No. Be mindful about the amount of television you watch. Only when I reach a higher level of spirituality, can I watch without being influenced.

There are many police dramas on television, filled with violence and destruction. When you consistently watch shows with such destruction, be aware of the comedy of errors taking place. This is not the type of world you want to believe exists. Look at them with laughter and possibly compassion or consider restricting such forms of entertainment.

What benefit is it to you if you believe that the earth is filled with destruction and violence? You be the judge of this one.

Be aware that you are always planting something within your mind. There are times when you may want to run from something that had in the past continually caused fear within you. What Holiness wants is for you to know that nothing can really threaten your real existence. Many of us on the spiritual path come up against our past beliefs and have gained the courage and spiritual fortitude to let them go.

Abundance

Let's talk about the concept of abundance, as we learn to treat our minds in such a way that we attract better good into our lives including money. For example, we can obtain more of the good of God by simply aligning our minds with the mind of God. A simple treatment may go as follows:

"The mind of God is naturally abundant.
My mind is a part of the mind of God. I am
therefore naturally abundant."

All of us need things to **operate in this world. It is difficult to operate in scarcity and resort to "fake" real happiness. Scarcity is simply one of those** beliefs of the body's eyes. You have the abundance of God that Holiness will simply shower you with as you work for Holiness. Therefore you are not to let yourself live in scarcity.

You do not need to go looking for this abundance; it will find its way to you. You will actually be guided to it. Scarcity is one of those worldly beliefs that Holiness wants us to let go of. Hear this again. *Scarcity is a belief. It has no truth in the mind of God.* The mind of God is naturally and completely abundant. It is an infinite abundance.

The error that most of us were taught is that our jobs, our businesses or some physical thing supplies us. It is Holiness that supplies us as we turn from these limiting sources of supply to an unlimited view. We do these things, but they are not considered our source. As you view yourself as an unlimited-spiritual being, you begin to live by grace. This is the graciousness of Holiness. You do not earn its goodness by doing something, you already have it. Accept the goodness by expressing yourself, but do not assign anything as your source other than Holiness.

Applies Across the Board to All Issues
As a matter of fact, this method of treatment is effective for many of the things that plague the mind of humans. God has no fear. God has no anger. God has no anxieties. Treat your mind appropriately and purposefully about these things and release them. Be very firm with your mind on these things.

If you do this you cannot help but be successful. You must remember that when you treat your mind, you have all the power of heaven behind you. These worldly beliefs are not to hinder you in any way.

Note that you are simply aligning your mind with the mind of God. How could you possibly not be successful with that?

Now you have been given the Science of Mind or New Thought trinity, which is summarized as follows:

- The conscious part of the mind is that which you think with and is planting seed thoughts through your thinking.
- The subconscious mind is the part that executes the plantings. This part accepts the seeds and grows what you think about. If you choose to believe something, the subconscious will seek to support your beliefs whether they are true or not.
- The only part that you see is the result of these plantings and that is body or physical creation.

It should be noted that in many parts of this writing the intent is to combine both heart and mind. Some references to keeping the heart open really say that this part of the mind is open and allowed to flourish. Since the heart knows, let it make decisions. It is through this heart that God is reached. It is through this heart where we experience our Holiness. The Holy Spirit lives in your subconscious. This is your heart.

The Christian or Bible Trinity

The Second Trinity we discuss is the Bible Trinity, which is the Father, Son, and Holy Spirit. It is similar to the earlier trinity. There again are three parts and each part is very powerful. Here we give each part a somewhat human description. This is not accurate, yet like the soil example given previously these are parables that the reader must use to understand principle.

In this trinity each part is invisible to the human eye. That is, the Father is God and is a spirit. The Holy Spirit can be called the Mother Principle of Life and is also a spirit. The Son is the created life of God and again is a spirit. Try to think of these three beings to be like a smoke filled room. The particles of smoke are floating together, and may come from three distinct fires, yet the smoke cannot be distinguished by its source. Here the attempt is for you to understand oneness. All the power and energy of God is contained in each part. Yet the parts are not separate. All are in a heavenly state of unity.

Other names for the Son are Jesus, the Christ, or You. Yes, please understand that God only created one life. Some call this life the son. For purposes of this writing the son is just the only life God created. You claim your spiritual power and correct relationship to creation by accepting yourself as the Son of God or created life of God regardless of which gender you seem to occupy in your body. In particular, gender does not matter. We simply have a habit of seeing things from our human perspective which is unfortunately most times a duality and an inappropriate label.

God as First Cause
God is the first part of the trinity. Though often depicted as male, this is not necessary. This is the creator of all and of course existing within all. This is love and all that is created is made from the fabric of love. This Being has such names as the Cos-

mos, the Universe, the Unified Field and Allah. Regardless of the name you give this Being or the way you try to describe it, you cannot completely define or confine it. Certainly any physical description is simply insufficient.

God is perfect and cannot perceive error. It cannot see the world that we appear to live in although its partner spirit, the Holy One has been given the job of merging heaven and earth. Therefore God maintains the perfection of its universe by just having the ability to only see perfection. I remember the first time I read that said that God cannot see my body or my affairs. This made no sense to me, yet I was curious. I also remember a classmate who was reading the same thing and became very sad about this. It seemed so impersonal. It is also at variance with the common belief that God knows everything.

A very popular mystic, Joel Goldsmith who I have a great deal of respect for was one of the first writers who introduced me to this concept of God not being aware of our dream state. A mystic is one who without a process just knows. I am able to channel information in this way now. Yet, it makes sense to me when I look at the madness of the earthly plane, it must be suggested that God has nothing to do with it. Otherwise, it conflicts with my understanding of a loving and compassionate God.

Sometimes we attempt to better describe a thing by looking at its opposite. Yet what is opposite to all? One such attempt is the feeling of fear which is considered the opposite of God or the absence of love. Some have attempted to use the word hate as the opposite of love. Again these are at best attempts to describe something that has no description. Add any attempt to logically confine these terms and we just add to the confusion.

At one time while teaching a group of preteens, from ages 10 to 13, the question of love came up. One child made the statement that "love is the most fearful thing I can think of." When asked why, she said that it is completely out of control. A person loses control completely when they are in love. It is for this reason that one can be completely afraid of love. Loss of control is dealing in the unknown.

Some of the things that come to mind are the absence of logical thinking and the blindness that love engenders. All of these are referring to that feeling of infatuation that arises in romantic love. Yet, this same irresponsibility and blindness can be said about a mother who smothers her child under the excuse of love. This may be called a high level of attachment and possibly some fear. It is often called love.

While taking my two girls to the doctor one day the doctor noticed the awkwardness when telling her that I was a stay at home dad. She remarked that I one day would appreciate this position as studies show that men are wonderful caregivers because of their ability to raise children with a greater level of detachment. These children are more self confident and perform better in school.

It has turned out that my two girls are doing exceptionally well as teenagers, yet they also have an exceptional mother. Though as Dad, I took care of the household and their daily care through the early years of their lives. During the time of raising my girls I had a spiritual practice. I therefore state that this practice guided the development of my children. Give God more of your attention through spiritual practice and see that guidance comes. You may not be aware of it, yet through prayer, practice, and study of God, you are being guided. My preference is to praise God.

It should be said that God sometimes *seems* so detached from us as humans. Yet it is my belief that God maintains the universe in absolute order. Otherwise, God is uncaring and unconcerned with me. In form, I see opportunities to believe this.

My choice is to call my partner spirit the Holy Spirit. One can call it God if they desire. It operates as if it were God. Yet the difference is so miniscule that it doesn't matter. The trinity of the Bible recognizes this being as a spirit created by God

An important point that must be made about God and the trinity being described here is that everything God created is fully whole. This means that the Holy Spirit and the Christ are both fully God. All of God's creations are like God; they are fully God or whole.

Contrast this with humans who are seeking to grow spiritually. We too are fully God, yet we are learning to turn away from our human training to become aware of who we really are. God's creations do not need to grow. The Christ and the Holy Spirit know what they are and easily display incredible power, peace, and joy.

The Holy Spirit

This can be considered the Mother Principle of Life. She was created by God to guide you the child of God to your fullness. The Holy One is really God's answer to the creation of an ego.

At creation the child was given all power and since the child does not know the range of its power the Holy Spirit must assist the child to fruition. While the child is the Christ, please do not think of the Christ as a novice. The Holy Spirit is for you who don't know that you are the Christ. You are the novice. It is within your thinking where you can become mature. This means that you must leave all your major decisions to the Holy One. The Holy One makes no mistakes and cannot become confused.

Think of yourself as a body that does not know that it is an all-powerful spirit. The Holy Spirit has been given the duty of assisting you primarily in the return to your Christ nature. Yet, the Holy One also seems to have a limit. *It will not assist without your conscious request.* You have been given complete freedom to even make mistakes, yet the Holy One will clean up your mistakes and bring a Holiness to them as well if you just request such help. This Holy Spirit will teach you about love and how to really bring a level of care to all your relations if you will just allow it to do so.

All the power of God is within the Holy One. Yet, unlike God, the Holy One works on the world of illusion through your mind. The world of illusion is the world of in which we see; yet we have the choice of believing in it. It is like we are asleep and living in a dream world and do not know it. Such humans as Jesus, Buddha, and Krishna are believed to have taken full control of their power by awakening. These are children of God like each of us who simply awakened from a dream state when they allowed the Holy Spirit to become their guide through life.

These three along with others still exist in the realm of the Kingdom and come into our minds in the way that we can understand them. Each focuses on a culture that understands them. Yet each is in the Holy One.

Pray as if the Holy One is the only one you are praying to. This Being can help you see your errors and erroneous judgments. It, like God is very gentle, just, and generous. The recommendation is that you seek out the Holy One and give yourself fully to this being as your guide by saying yes to it.

For example, you can look into the unknown areas of your soul and just say, "yes" to this unknown. Do not be like the child, who believed that love is fearful. You may feel this fear as well, yet you know that this is not the nature of love or the Holy One. Say "yes" boldly and courageously that you trust love to see those unknown areas of your soul. This requires that you fully understand that the Holy One is perfect love beyond human comprehension. Say" yes" to perfect love because of the nature of perfect love. Stay close by "knowing that you live, move, and have your being in God[4]."

When you know the nature of perfect love, it begins to make your life more beautiful. It makes no errors if given full sway. Otherwise you just struggle with an ever changing world and resist the change. *Know that the Holy One is with you and it becomes easier to live by grace.*

The past cannot be our teacher. Any lesson one pulls out of his/her experience is not a lesson of the Holy Spirit. The Holy One is always present with us and through that awareness we learn. Our past experience calls upon another teacher that we do not want. There is test that we can use to measure if our learning is true. That is the test of perfect peace. The following is an excerpt from A Course in Miracles:

If you are wholly free of fear of any kind, and those who meet or even think of you share your perfect peace, then you can be sure that you have learned God's lesson and not your own. Unless all of this is true there are dark lessons in your mind that hurt and hinder you and everyone around you.... Do not be concerned about how you can learn a lesson so completely different from everything that you have taught yourself... Your part is very simple. You only recognize that everything that you have taught yourself you do not want. Ask to be taught...[5]

You are with the Holy One to bring your whole world to a state of peacefulness through your learning. Note that this test of perfect peace encompasses your entire world, you affect your whole world because of *how you think creates your world.* If you have friends or family that you are in touch with who are currently experiencing difficulties, just call upon the Holy One to strengthen your peace as you learn and situations will magically improve. Do not attempt to tell your friends, what you are learning or try to teach them what you are learning. The Holy One encompasses them and is more aware of them and you than you can imagine. Focus on what you are learning from your teacher. Begin to learn by becoming empty of beliefs. *Begin to willingly not know.* Of course a time arrives very quickly where you do know.

Our personal task is to bring our personal world to a state of peace. Once we do that we can personally live in a place of peace. This is once again placing personal responsibility with each of us. In this way the entire planet earth will eventually reach that state of peace. There is nothing outside of you as you are a spirit. Actually you are the spirit and the spirit encompasses everything then all of reality is attached through this spirit. Spiritual development suggests that these are ideas that must be nurtured and grown. You are divinizing your world.

The Son

You are the Son. The Son is the only child of God. It is created life that encompasses both the male and female principles of life. It was once thought that holy books like the Bible were written using male language because of male dominated societies. That may have been true. However this writing is saying that Son should be interpreted as created life which encompasses both genders. Each of us has both energies within us. For that reason we are like our parentage. A better term for Son is really child of God or child. Each of us is that child of God. I stay with the word Son because this is the biblical term. For the women of this world I must accept that child is a better term. Child only denotes something the parent created and God only extends itself such that Christ is fully God.

Now in understanding that there is just one created life of God we must again leave the world of effects. This is a spiritual principle and keeps us out of the duality of male and female, and from the friction of machismo or feminist thinking. As a writer I can avoid such terms as he/she or it to explain a person in this section. Many have a problem of describing themselves or God as an "It." This is understandable, yet if you use the term "issue" or "problem" too often, it simply means that you have to work on forgiveness. It is not your place to have too many issues or problems in situations.

Therefore, Son is created life. It is all powerful. It is the Christ principle of life and all of us can attain it by allowing our wonderful guide to lead the way. This really is not easy, yet it is simple. The courage of "letting" as opposed to "doing or making" something happen must be adhered to. It is easier to float with the stream as opposed to swimming upstream against the current. These are some powerful currents and we age pre-maturely if we resist them.

The following definition of the Christ as the only Son of God is offered from the *Science of Mind Textbook*.[6]

Christ, The Word of God manifest in and through man. In a liberal sense, the Christ means the Entire Manife-

station of God and is, therefore, the Second Person of the Trinity. Christ is Universal Idea, and each one "puts on the Christ" to the degree that he surrenders a limited sense of Life to the Divine Realization of wholeness and unity with Good, Spirit, God.

The Son lives in a mind that is God. This son creates like God by thinking correctly. I control the conditions of my life by being careful about letting my mind stray down certain paths. Generally, these paths must be considered neutral which means that my mind does not stray into the past or future or seek to judge. It stays in the *now* to access the pure thoughts of God. Otherwise the thoughts of the past or the uncertainty of the future dominate the mind. The past may have good things, yet it also has the potential of regrets. The future may be hopeful, yet it also has the potential of worry about uncertainty. The present is more real and has neither of these things.

The seamless space of heaven is here. It helps us understand why mystics for years spoke in such strange terminology. My gift to you my beloved is that you simply open your heart to truth. Leave room for your teacher to enter, so that you can open more fully to it. Ancient documents are being brought forward by modern day mystics like you and me.

A mind is nothing other than thoughts. Therefore everything in my life is some aspect of my thought system. All things are ideas that have taken form. I have a choice of accepting these ideas as good or bad. It is probably better to just cease judging them and label them neutral because I desire to experience more positive things in my life. Many beliefs are replaced with truth. This is especially true about the other human beings that come into my experience. Habitually, I must accept them as an aspect of my own Holiness.

For example, if someone tells you that they are poor and cannot pay their rent. You can help without saying a word by denying this supposed reality that they are experiencing. Your place is to see them as whole as this is the condition of the Sonship. It is one. Your compassion for the experience that the person is having is acceptable. Yet your real place is to accept the Sonship as whole and without verbally saying a word. Just think about the real condition of the Sonship. It is perfect. If you agree that life is hard and that person is poor, you are sinning and unable to forgive what you are seeing and hearing. Just be willing to forgive what you are being told and think about the reality of what God created and you have placed another vision there.

You may later be surprised at what happens. Unless you are able and willing to give sufficient money to each person who approaches you in this way, lean on spiritual truth and let God be God. In this way you spiritually gossip beautifully. God is planted in truth within your mind. At least you do not agree with erroneous statements and strengthen falsity. It is your thinking that these thoughts become heavenly and holy.

Of course you can never really plant God anywhere other than in your own awareness. This simply means that you are choosing to remember God at all times. You are choosing to remember truth. Understand that the truth does not need your protection. It is the lies that are being found in your consciousness. There is no one to correct other than yourself.

As a child of God you can grow to learn of the tremendous power that you have available to you. The following story is provided to give an example.

A past client came to me one day and told me that she was having trouble sleeping. I recall telling her that she should send me a text the next time that happens and I will take care of it. My phone is usually on the nightstand next to my bed when I am asleep. The phone also makes a short beep when I receive a text. To tell the truth, I had no idea why I said that or what I would do. I simply told her not to call me and that I would not call her. I would simply help her to sleep after receiving the text.

About three days later I received a text from her. I recall that it was about four in the morning and I was sound asleep. I just heard my phone beep and I looked at it. It was from Gloria and the text read, "I cannot sleep and feel awful."

After reading this I did a little process that took me about three seconds and I immediately went back to sleep.

The next day while reading my emails, I noted one from Gloria. Her email was poorly written and did not really make sense to me. I did note that she was thanking me for something. Since I did not understand the writing, I decided to call her.

"Gloria, I just read the email from you and I do not understand what you are saying," was my comment.

"I was so excited after the wonderful and peaceful sleep I experienced that I did not take the time to calm myself before sending that email," was her response.

"So, you were really writing me to thank me for helping you sleep."

"Yes, immediately after sending the text I fell into a deep and wondrously comfortable sleep. It was like you immediately drugged me."

"I am grateful for your words then. I just didn't understand your email."

I do remember what I did after seeing her text that night. I remember picking up the phone and reading her text. Then I said: "Peace be still!"

I then put the phone down and went back to sleep. My phone emits a light and I recall turning the cell phone on its face so that I would not be disturbed by the light it emits.

Do you now understand what a child of God can do? A child of God can help others and do anything. You my beloved are a child of God. You are not simply a body. You are a beautiful and powerful state of awareness and you can literally move mountains for yourself and others if you begin to believe this. Like me you will have flashes of this power. You consistently avail yourself of this power by staying aware of it with feeling.

In this above example, I had awakened myself from a sleep for about ten seconds to help a friend. I did not think. I just did it. You can do the same. We are of one being. Each of us is of God. We learn to deal with situations in consciousness.

To summarize the second trinity:
- God is the creator of all life and is first in the Christian trinity.
- Holy Spirit is second in this trinity and is the guide for the child and the voice for God. This spirit is in your mind as the connecting link to God.
- Third in this trinity is the child or Christ. This has been called the son of God, yet it is really a created life of God which has no gender.

Never have I read a single book that has focused its attention on the Holy Spirit. Yet the Holy Spirit has all power on earth and in heaven at its disposal. Its primary purpose is to help you become clear that you are the Christ. It has no ego goals. For that reason most humans do no focus on it. The Science of Mind trinity seems to have as its focus an explanation of how things are created in the world of form. For that reason it seems to occupy those minds that want things in the world of form.

This is not criticizing those who want things. The writer had to learn to just *want more God*. Since God is everything, there is no such thing as more God.

There is such a thing as more awareness of God's presence. This relieves the mind of the conflict of wanting the things of this world and having to make them happen. Literally one can learn that by believing in the power of God, one will be cared for. If I believe I am a body, I then believe that I must use this body to make things happen. If I learn to trust my spirit, I am led to the real source of power even in this world of effects.

The Third Trinity
The Third Trinity is that of Mind, Body, and Spirit. In this trinity we deal with the healing of the world and the return of sense. This trinity is very personal and of tremendous benefit.

- Your Mind is the first part of this Trinity. This is again the conscious part of you that you control. Like the First Trinity, this is the part where you often do your plantings. However, it is this part where your ego lives and is capable of ruling you with vengeance. There will be more to read of this ego in a later chapter of this book.

- Your Spirit is the second part of this trinity. This part is perfect and is the home of the Holy Spirit, God, and the Christ. It is often called the subconscious mind, the kingdom of heaven, or simply God. God reigns supreme in this part of you and extends itself throughout your spirit in a way that there is not a discordant thought that arises in your spirit. All that exists in this part of you is love. Peace is also a prominent aspect of this part of mind.

- Your Body is the third part of this trinity. Your body is where you experience the physical world and the physical universe. This physical world is neither positive nor negative. It is neutral. That which is in your consciousness determines whether your body is healthy or not.

As shown in the First Trinity, the plantings of the conscious mind flow into the subconscious mind and form is created. However, in this Third Trinity the desire is to severely limit the planting of what the conscious mind creates so that the creation that comes from the subconscious mind is all that is desired. This also limits the ego from domination over physical creation.

We limit the ego by living in the now and allowing no past or future thoughts to dominate our mind. The person now has a very healthy body that learns only from spirit. The ego does not come into the now. Creation proceeds from a much lessened ego structure, absolving the ego of its power as creation proceeds under the full direction of love. All selfishness is gone and miracles abound. Since a sick mind is what sickens a body, when the mind has healed the body is healed. It is then able to serve the spirit. We merge spirit and mind to heal.

The Kingdom of Heaven on Earth
Now the time has come for Heaven to take over earth bringing lasting peace. Heaven and earth no longer exist as separate states and we experience a joy and peace that cannot be described. We are all seen as God and treat one another as such. One must understand that the kingdom of heaven is God's creation and really *is everything*. With Heaven as the sole ruler, the mind heals and no longer receives ego plantings. All live in the peace of God.

Your true powers lie in your abilities to create. Creation happens in the formless and those are the patterns that attach to species and those with common characteristics or thought patterns. Creation happens with correct knowledge. This is how God thinks. This is what God knows. The Holy Spirit can be considered as the subconscious. It simply is interpreting truth and bringing forth what you are willing to see. We do somewhat personalize it. It is considered a joyous personality. Joy is productive. It is gracious.

True creation does not judge based upon form. Remember the energy field that has each of us attached. These thoughts can be picked up anywhere. Bless those who pray as they have learned the necessity of holy contact.

This chapter has attempted to explain three ways of looking at the trinity. They are similar, yet they have differences. Hopefully you see how each explains creation, and the benefit of understanding all three. Seek to understand each and be provided lessons in mind training. In this way one can grow quickly into a most beneficial presence.

Begin to understand that the two spiritual entities are like me. I am not a body. I am the blessed Son regardless of what gender my appearance suggests, or what my eyes or my past has told me. *Son just means created life. It is like an energy field that is everywhere. You are this energy field.* Both the Holy One and the Great Creator are like my parents, and they instill in me more truth as I grow and they love me gently, beautifully, and completely. That love includes anything I could ever want or need.

I did not create myself and have parents who desire to give everything to me. That gift was given at my creation. It is already done. I have been given heaven. Jesus called it the kingdom of heaven. Call it what you will. It is home and it contains God and the Holy One. These parents want me to return to their embrace and they desire more of my attention. As I give them my attention, it is like I am in consciousness returned to my home in God and love blesses me so sweetly. Another way of looking at this is I have been living in the world of form. God and the Holy Spirit want to teach me about eternity and as I learn about eternity my life improves as eternity has gifts that I can use.

Summary and Use of the Three Trinities

The Christian Trinity of God, Son, and Holy Spirit tell me where I stand in that order. I am the Son.

Please understand that these three beings encompass everything. Nothing is outside these three.

Use the Science of Mind Trinity to plant proper ideas in your mind. This is done through affirmations and prayer. Learn that as the Son of God you must plant some of the qualities that you desire, if you are not experiencing them. Begin to affirm what you want, such as "I am strong. I am peace." Plant these affirmations in your mind, water them with continuous use and allow them to strengthen your beliefs.

The Third Trinity is used to understand what I must concentrate on for improvements in my life. Since the mind is the only part of me that can get sick, it is necessary that I clean up my mind to experience a greater degree of wellness. This wellness includes my physical body and the body of my affairs. A healed mind experiences a wonderful life. There is no other way to use the term salvation or enlightened.

Allow the joy of Holiness to be yours right now. Heaven is at your doorstep and within your touch. Experience this now and decide not to await death of the body.

CHAPTER SEVEN

Complete Reliance upon God

Suppose I am operating from a state of fear. Well I have every right to do so. It may not be fun or healthy, yet there is a good reason to be fearful. That reason is because I am relying upon myself to operate. If I believe in my humanness, I should be fearful if I believe that the human can resolve things for me. That human simply is not perfect. Since I have a choice of relying on something that is perfect or relying on the imperfect and have chosen the imperfect, there is good reason to be fearful. Why stay in such a position?

Why not change this way of living to rely solely on God or God's teacher the Holy Spirit? Here I begin to rely upon perfection. The only requirement from me is to continue to make this choice and find the patience to accept the outcome. The outcome is certain to be acceptable, however I must learn this.

Humanly we learn to believe what we see. From this consciousness we respond to our beliefs and interpretations as opposed to reality. Turn your cheek and accept that love is present and respond truly. Each is asking for love or giving love. Seek to recognize this in each instance and love will assist.

One cannot live in fear. It is neither a motivator nor a teacher. One can only recognize fear and allow love to surface. Fear is a call for love. Recognize fear as this alone. Fear does not exist. Love is everything.

I am lost within a maze and do not know the way out. Getting out is *spiritual emancipation.* It is my desire to find my way out. However, I am within it. Consider if I were to ask someone who knows the sure path to the exit. If this is what I want, why not ask this person who is above the maze and can see all the paths?

Whether one accepts this or not, each is completely dependent upon God. This requires humility. This humility can be private such that I don't need to admit it if I believe humility is weakness. It is not weakness. It just is. It is the meek that shall inherit the earth. They shall because they know their real source. Another reason is because I as a body don't really exist. This is just one of the experiences I am having in my mind. The body is part of the illusion. I cannot depend upon my way of thinking which started when I thought I was a body.

Building Treasures in Heaven

During his famous sermon on the mount, Jesus made the following statement: "Build not treasures on earth where moth, rust, and thieves dwell. But build up for you, treasures in heaven.[7]" These treasures are my truths or my accurate thoughts. We live within a mind that takes the impression from our thoughts and continually gives us back a representation of that impression.

Consider a person who is constantly acquiring things. They are saving for retirement, continually improving the value of their home, and seeking to "make it" as this term signifies. They are very worldly. This is not necessarily a criticism. It just describes how many of us seek to be successful.

A person who lives this way is building up treasures on earth. The earth is all this person believes in and they cannot be faulted for this. This experience of earth is very appealing and convincing. It is easy to believe that we live on earth and must make the best of it. This is not considered selfish nor is it wrong. All of us make choices based upon what we believe.

Have you heard the word "airhead" before? This is a term given to a person who is without any substance. Can you fault a person for being this way? It really is an inaccurate judgment. Everyone is a creation of God. Unfortunately we tend to judge one another. Operating from this standpoint we first want to know what is the truth that we rely and operate under. Keep things simple. God is truth. Peace is truth. Love is truth. Since I already have all this within me, I need not seek to continually acquire knowledge.

Alternatively, we could seek to build up treasures in heaven, which means that we begin to believe God's truths. Staying aware of truth can be difficult in a world of ego domination. We study continuously, to keep the mind involved in truth.

My responses to others allow God to respond to me. This is something that I continually practice.

Our Treasures are Our Truth

Heaven is a state of consciousness. Therefore we are to build a state of consciousness based upon truths. Our job is to let go and surrender our current beliefs. This state of consciousness cares for us and all of our affairs. This means that our entire world finds a state of peace and joy. Since the world is the world of our minds, everyone we are in relationship with will enjoy this state of peace and joy.

Now suppose one tenth of the people on the planet accept their state of consciousness. This means that the other nine tenths of the world are affected. We don't have to have a close relationship with others to be affected by this consciousness. Simply, we will not come in contact with anyone who is unaffected because our minds have made this impossible. This is why each of us is so powerful. *God is within our minds.* We therefore have the power of God at our disposal. Yet this requires humility because our humanly existence still tries to tell us otherwise.

It is this belief in a humanly existence that has no power. I am not able to determine when my human self is operating or when I am grounded in love. Therefore my power is unavailable to me. By humbly seeking to get out of the way (getting that human out of the way) I witness the divine at work. This means that I learn the power of observation.

Surrender
Learn the power of surrendering your life to the whole. Here are a few points in the process.
-live in the now
-avoid too much goal orientation
-pray for daily guidance
-share your ideas where you can

Living in the now is simply keeping your thoughts in the present. I once noted that I was more present after a meditation exercise bringing more focus to whatever I was doing.

Certainly having no life plans is contrary to what most believe. It has been stated in the soil example that the fertile field of your mind may grow weeds. Grow confidence in Holiness's direction. It knows how to guide, protect and take care of you.

Sharing ideas and truth is the way that you grow faith and mental strength. You share ideas by thinking properly about everyone you meet, regardless of their circumstances. Everyone is a child of a most wonderful God and you must remember this regardless of what your eyes or ears tell you. Become a teacher of truth. This is one of the main purposes of this writing. The teacher and student strengthen mentally when these truths are accepted.

Emotional Power

Right behind my heart is a nerve center called the solar plexus. I learned about the solar plexus while studying Karate many years ago. We were taught to punch someone in the chest just to the right of the heart to disable them. Years later I read about this area as the center of the body's feeling nature. Since the heart is just a muscle that pumps blood, the feelings that are ordinarily attributed to feelings of the heart, are wrong. The heart gets more credit just because it is noisy and seems to be the center of life within the body. Consider this as a parable where one is the noisy conscious mind, which is constantly thinking and providing information to you. This noisy person can be considered the heart.

The other part is the subconscious mind. It makes no sound, yet it really is the doer that causes the seed thoughts and beliefs that have been planted to grow. The subconscious is like the solar plexus in that it makes no sound, yet is really the center of the nature of feelings. All emotions flow through this solar plexus and the solar plexus responds to them. Yet these emotions also affect the outside. The body is not to be ignored.

When I was a sophomore in high school I was a sprinter on the track team. My primary race was the 440 yard run. Running track requires a great deal of practice and discipline. It requires the willingness to endure great pain to reach the high level of endurance required for success. The times of exhaustion and pain came immediately after the expenditure of tremendous physical and emotional energy.

I was about 15 years old and during track season we trained every day. There were numerous track meets and we were given many opportunities to compete against other schools in the area.

Every day, my track coach timed my races during practice to give me a measure of my performance. Coach told me that I would learn of the incredible differences between my practice speeds for the 440 yard run, and the competitive speed I could run during the outside track meets. The primary difference was that my body responded to competition and performed by running faster than in the practice runs. In order to take advantage of the rush of emotional power that was available to me it was necessary that I tap into this power.

During practice, I'd run very hard for the first 380 yards of the 440-yard run. The last 60 yards I would give my all so that I could finish the run at full speed.

However, Coach told me that I should run hard beginning at the 350-yard mark because the extra power my body gave me from the endorphins that allow the heart to beat faster pumping blood and extra nutrients to all parts of the body during a competitive track meet.

At the time Coach told me, it made no sense to me. During practice, if I turned to full power early I would practically fall flat on my face at the end of the race due to fatigue. I also wanted to reserve some strength in case there was another runner in front of me or right next to me. I certainly didn't want to be fatigued such that I was unable to finish the competition.

It took several track meets for me to learn of the additional strength available to me due to the competitive events. It was necessary to trust both my body and my coach. Due to the heavy training during the track season, I was able to build strength and endurance. My planning for each race changed as I got stronger. Near the end of my sophomore year, I began to run the entire race at nearly 100% of full power and my race time improved considerably.

Running track showed the emotions that flowed through my body added considerable power to my body. While we had team practice, this paled by comparison to the strength and endurance that I created during a track meet. A competitor must assume that they will be stronger during a competitive event. In an earlier chapter the example was given of a woman picking up a car. This is similar. It speaks to the tremendous emotional power that is available in certain circumstances.

Suppose you have a friend named John who is standing about twenty feet from you. Now suddenly a stranger approaches John and slaps him very hard in the face such that John falls to the ground in pain.

Now this stranger turns and walks in your direction. Your heart begins to beat faster; your body starts to emit endorphins such that puts your body into a state of readiness. For a few seconds your body actually gets stronger as it prepares for an assault. The stranger walks past you and keeps walking. Your heartbeat slows and you begin to relax. Your body can become stronger, or weaker through fear. All of this depends upon your mental composition.

While the heartbeat sends additional nutrients to all parts of the body, it is the solar plexus that starts this process after the body perceives a need. It is the endorphins that speed up the heartbeat. The whole point here is to begin to *understand the strength of feelings*. Whether the elevated feelings are necessary or not, this is where real strength is available to both the body and your affairs. This is where conviction is available. It is also where real peace and joy which in combination brings about that state of bliss.

Feelings are the Software of Your Soul.
The soul is my real identity. This software causes my entire world to operate a certain way. Yet my only job is to become aware of these things. The soul is unchanging and unchangeable. With awareness, I make the decision to bring my outer world in harmony with my inner world by desiring peace which is the defining quality of your soul. The solar plexus can be considered a nerve center of my soul in some respects.

When I first became a spiritual practitioner, I noticed that some people seek to elevate their feelings by praying with a great deal of feeling. There is nothing wrong with this; however, this is how I judged the way some people pray when they pray aloud. There is a lot of power in my feelings. Yet, this conviction is also available with just an awareness of what is true. Then letting the truth takes place. The truth does not need defending nor does it need strengthening. I state and affirm truth in prayer or in my journaling.

Anyone can grow truth in his or her awareness simply by being aware of truth. The physical form does have some power, yet the examples given of emotional power literally can wear the body out. I don't need or want these endorphins rushing through my body continually. They more commonly arise through fears and things that I really don't want. Peace is more desirable.

Cleaning the Mind
There was a minister I knew who taught that one must treat the mind like a pail of muddy water. Place a water hose in the muddy water to clear up

the mud. Eventually the clean water is all that will remain in the pail.

I state truths to myself as affirmations. This helps to clear up untruths that may be driving my life. Another way to be is still and let the Holy One tell me what is true. When I ask, she responds. This is her desire and function. Recognize her by building this relationship. Give the teacher a chance to come alive within. She will teach of her peace. She will teach of the incredible love she has for us. She will tell of a purpose and will suggest things to work on.

Agree with The Holy One
However, if she suggests anything, just be sure to be in agreement. No matter how impossible it may seem, just agree. Then we have the chance of proving that nothing is impossible. Then the Holy One makes sure that whatever is agreed upon just happens. My agreement is willingness to let Holiness do what it does. It just gives and never takes anything away.

She is a peaceful teacher. She always finds peaceful ways of solving any problem. With our human mind we sometimes feel that we must meet situations head on. Yet given an opportunity, the teacher of peace proves the value and power of peace. This is how the meek inherit the earth; [9] they have this ability to let their humility take over the earth as they know it. This is because they learn to let the Holy One stay in the driver's seat.

Therefore peace is one of the primary treasures that are to be built in my heavenly mind. As my affairs take on this quality, my world matches and joy becomes evident. The Holy One is sometimes referred to as the teacher of peace. I am entirely dependent upon this Being for my livelihood. As God's representative, it is here that my total dependence on God lies.

I once met an herbalist who told me that a person can practically eat poison and the body will not be affected if the mind can remain joyous. It does mean that joy has a healing quality. Again we come back to the term healing.

My suggestion is to find the joy that is not based upon any external circumstance. This is that joy that wells up from within. There is a spiritual process that begins with the desire for peace of mind. It is not a peace that the world can give you. It is called a perfect peace. From this peace an inner joy arises. Following is perfect health.

While I do consider myself to have a logical mind, many who possess logical minds will not understand this. I have learned that the logical mind is usually a separate mind. Admittedly there are times when I stop and ask myself what day of the week it is. Yet, this is OK. It is fine to have that idea that I am being directed by something that I cannot fully describe. This something really loves me and somehow keeps me happy. It really is averse to my past way of thinking. I understand that the natural state of the mind is abstract.

There are times when my mind feels very abstract. It just doesn't feel or appear coherent. Yet it is natural to feel a little abstract at times, all I have to do is *remember that God is present and let God be God.*

Mental Abstraction

Throughout this book are discussions on mental abstraction. It is just the opposite of a judgmental mind. It is a mind that lets go as opposed to seeking to say how things should be. It knows that all is as it should be. It is a mind that is not so affected by what the eyes see.

Patience and Peace are Directors.
These are again eternal qualities and cannot be changed. Remember that the eternal is what I begin to esteem. Otherwise I can easily get caught in form.

Many beautiful teachers have taught of the form-less and speak consistently of the spiritual. The problem is that many try to convert what is spiri-tual into the physical and get confused.

Jesus for example said that he would teach with pa-rables. There is a bad habit of many spiritual read-ers to attempt to convert the spiritual into the phys-ical. Your job is to understand what is spiritual and begin to esteem the spiritual. This is who you are. Begin to love, esteem and accept that all is spirit. Love all, and let it be. Do not seek to change it. God will not intrude upon my space nor will God seek to teach me unless I ask to be taught. Consistently asking to be taught is how I gain the consistent help of my Holiness. I will later discuss how Holiness is what I am.

There are many spiritual lessons in the Bible that teach spiritual truth. Most try to convert these spiritual lessons into the physical and get confused. Let these lessons be spirit and seek to just understand them with spirit. I must learn to raise my consciousness to the level of spirit to understand. I have that ability. Otherwise I just stay in the physical and stay confused as an ego.

Find Perfect Peace

That is all that is required. Perfect peace equals perfect health. You can see this more easily when thinking about the feeling of stress. When stress increases in your life, you begin to see how it tears up your body. Now consider a perfect peace. Consider a consistent feeling of "everything is just fine." The body heals through a consistent peace of mind.

An Unhappy Time

There was a time in my life when I had an unhappy thought within me. Now I admit that there were some circumstances that were unpleasant at the time. I remembered that thoughts create things. Therefore, I decided that I would begin to erase that ego idea that there was something wrong. Truth says that all there is, is God. Is my life outside of the mind of God? This was a defining moment for me. I had to remember it to stay on my spiritual growth path. God maintains perfection. My job is to get interested in and believe that this perfect life includes me. After years of suffering from depression and a long list of circumstances that can be demeaning and degrading, I just decided to let the truth take over my life. Unfortunately there are family members who do not understand that I have healed myself of that depression condition.

I even had a family member come to me and tell me that I should consider getting on some type of disability because I was not looking for a job. The truth is that many don't understand anyone who is on a spiritual growth plan. I heard her out, without comment.

There are people in my world who do not understand what I am doing. Each person on the spiritual path must understand that their life path will be anything but normal. There is no normal life path. Each of us are "coming out from among them" (some of you may have heard of that scripture). Following the Holiness path may seem a little different at times, but I must become comfortable with it. Consider this an aspect of the peace of God.

I hear my family and friends, but I really don't respond to judgments. I asked my daughter if she has ever sees me unhappy?

"I do admit that there seems to be something you are working on and I do not see you complaining about things. I know you are writing and this seems to give you a great deal of satisfaction," was her comment.

My oldest daughter has seen me rise the corporate ladder and later become a lover of God. She has seen a flower child and a rise in the corporate world. I love my family, but I will not be swayed by their opinions. This is not a popularity contest. While ill, there were many questions of when I would return to my corporate life. Through Holiness, I know what I am doing and as a result the family has experienced my love and attentiveness. They have also seen money arrive from unexpected sources.

I do remember that everyone and everything that comes into my awareness is a part of my thought system. Someone who doubts me may be an expression of my own inner doubt. I must not get upset with my doubters. This is my blessing. I learn to observe with awareness.

Path to Holiness

Holiness feeds, cloths, and takes care of its participants. It takes great spiritual discipline to spend time in meditation and silence to stay on your path. It is a learning to value Holiness and not to devalue it. The challenge is that it cannot be described. Yet, it is what you and I are. We are not to devalue ourselves. We are Holiness itself and as quickly as we learn this, as quickly we find that happiness has powerful friends.

In His famous Sermon on the Mount, Jesus says in the Lord's Prayer, "Give us this day our daily bread." Your daily bread comes through your prayer practices, which include meditation and whatever other practices you choose. Holiness somehow enters in and directs you specifically. A time does come when an obvious direction with the body and affairs becomes clear. There is no advice given here other than to *find the internal teacher*. This power provides for joy, peace, and well being.

The Rock of Spiritual Truth

In that same sermon Jesus spoke of the sinking sand. He is telling us not to build our lives on sinking sand. Anything other than Holiness is sinking sand. We are advised to build our lives on the rock of spiritual truth. We have built a house that withstands the rains and the storms. God can be counted on. *God only knows how to be God.* This means that God only knows how to love, perform miracles, and solve any situation considered to be difficult. God has no concept of size or difficulty.

Holiness exists within a perfect space of peace, including your joy and satisfaction. Nothing can touch it and nothing can disturb it. It is never late and meets every need. There is no resistance to Holiness.

A person must simply begin the process of finding inner peace. The universe awaits you. Are you next? *There is just one mind.* Allow that mind to blend into your mind until only the thoughts of God remain. What are those thoughts? This you must experience for yourself. Now you learn that "It is the power within that does the work."[10]

I am completely reliant upon God because separated from God I do not exist. When God created his child, God placed total love around and through the child. God simply expressed Itself and expanded to become a child of God. There is no separation between God and the child of God. It is my belief in separation and attendant responses from this belief that creates all difficulties.

This is my real existence. *As a child of God I am actually part of God.* I have no form as I am made in the image and likeness of God. As God has no form that can be described in the physical world, I have no form that can be described in the physical world. These statements also allow me to say that I was never born and will never die. I am a spirit that is infinite and forever. Claiming it will assist one in dealing with the concept of death.

Life then flows in my favor in all circumstances. This must be experienced. It is an easy and gracious way of living. It allows me to enjoy and express life almost effortlessly. It will then be understood that there really is no other way of living than living, moving, and having my beingness in God. I also experience the miraculous.

CHAPTER EIGHT

Ego

There is much controversy about the ego. The controversy is primarily about whether this ego is good or bad. Hopefully this can be cleared up in this chapter. First we must define the ego, which is a thought. It principally believes solely in forms. It is a thought of who you may think you are. For example many define themselves by what they do to make money. One might say that they are a lawyer or an electrician. We then attach positive or negative labels to these definitions. This way of looking at ourselves is so common that few question it.

If you can just remember that the ego is something you have created as a picture of yourself it can be better understood. You have mentally built a person and God did the same without an image. The two are not at war because Holiness does not fight. The ego may attempt to do so yet Holiness continues unabated. God ignores something it knows does not exist.

It may be a challenge to begin to believe that self-love of an ego is a growth of something you do not want. The controversy within some is that self love is always good. No one wants to believe that they have created monsters within them. Just let the thought be that we want to love what God created. The body and personality are to be under our care, but not worshipped.

Life's Labels

Most of us have many different labels. I have been a son to my mother, a husband to my wife, a father to my children, an employee to my manager at work, a manager to those who reported to me, and a coworker to other workers at my place of employment. Have you noticed one common characteristic of all these labels? They are all related to something else in our physical world. The labels also change based upon what we are doing at any given time.

Now begin to esteem or not esteem these labels by attaching values to them, they become confusing. A family member of mine had a period of unemployment and told me that he never wanted to be in that position again. He was full of fear, and there were no daily rituals in his life. Unemployment produced uncertainty and eliminated the daily ritual of going to work. Without daily ritual, many of us actually fall apart. Employment gives us things to do; it controls our ritualistic lives, and may give us values. Some jobs are held in higher esteem than others. Some without jobs feel a loss of self esteem. Jobs are also sometimes believed to be our primary source of income.

This world is constantly changing. How can we have any stability when the way we define ourselves is always changing? The physical world when looked at alone is in constant change. This makes sense, yet this writer (notice that I label myself as a writer because I am writing this at this moment) believes that we should learn to define ourselves more accurately. Nothing of this world is sufficient to explain to me what I am. I am not of this world. I am a spirit being endowed with all the blessings of my Holy Spirit.

Since God has no form, this also true about me. The only way I can learn of myself is to mentally deny all the terms that I once used to describe me. These terms can only tell me what I am not. There is no term that describes me or God.

Before going any further, let's summarize some **characteristics of ego thinking**:

- It is a belief about the self or who or what I think I am.
- It is based upon some other physical form. I am a husband to my wife.
- It changes over time, example: at this time I am a writer (or at this time I am writing a book).
- It has values attached to it (high or low esteem)

- It believes only in the physical as all its thoughts come from the physical.

If one were to take each of the five characteristics above and list the several hundred other characteristics that are related to these characteristics. Then one can get an idea of the tremendous complexity of this idea of ego.

How about we simplify all of this? Accept no worldly definition of yourself. You and I are not of this world. We are spirit. Can you now see why this ego definition can cause such havoc upon one's life? It is a personal definition that you created and can make so complex that it can become unmanageable. First, please understand that it is a thought that you get to accept or not. It doesn't matter whether someone else gives you their ideals or opinions. You get to make the decision whether you accept their thoughts or not.

The ego that you have created is not made in the spirit of love. Please understand the use of the word "you" in the previous sentence. This is necessary for each of us to accept responsibility for change. The ego was made out of fear and guilt. It is not something you want although it really does believe that it is a body. In your mind, you must *begin to accept that you are not a body or you may continue to side with your ego* and experience the limited desires of such a being. Now let's talk about some of the ways in which an ego operates.

For example, suppose you look at someone and decide that they are operating in their ego. What has really happened is that you have through your own ego seen something. An ego looks for other egos. A spirit looks for the spirit. Learn not to look at others through your ego, regardless of what they are doing. Improved health is one of the things that result from looking at others properly. We will deal with this more specifically later.

From the book The Power of Now[15] the following is a statement about the ego:

> *If they do not free themselves from their mind, they will be destroyed by it. They will experience increasing confusion, conflict, violence, illness, despair, madness. Egoic mind has become like a sinking ship. If you don't get off, you will go down with*

> *it. The collective egoic mind is the most dangerously insane and destructive entity to ever inhabit this planet.*

God's answer to your creation of an ego was the Holy Spirit. You choose who you are to serve. The Holy Spirit is a correct choice as this being leads you back to your true self which is God.

Adolph Hitler

Adolph Hitler has been given the title of the "worst person" of the twentieth century — credited with being cause of the holocaust as well as millions of deaths and the destruction of World War II. Yet, Adolph Hitler was one person who had characteristics that caused a nation to follow him. One might think that Hitler had a large ego. We could also attribute such characteristics to Mother Teresa or Mahatma Gandhi. One would normally believe that high self esteem is good.

Each of these persons operated within mind. Why it is that some are able to marshal larger movements than others? Is it the size of their egos that determine the number of people that they are able to affect? How can one measure the size of an ego in that it is just a thought?

The Adolph Hitler example is used to suggest that a large ego can be good or bad according to our judgment of it. Just understand that the ego is simply a belief that one has about himself or herself. That belief can change over time. Yet, there is another way to look at ego. It is sometimes called separation thinking. Anytime you use the outside world to create a self or ego, you have separated yourself from the whole. You have created a separate self.

Wholeness

In this view one is to consider themselves as whole. There is no definition of this, but it can just be called God. This is a spiritual concept and has no counterpart in the physical world. You must see yourself as spirit with no physical form. Yes, you are discounting the body that you appear to live in. As a spirit you are one with God and you have no physical description.

Seek to define yourself this way. Your actual belief will change at another point. This means that you may want to see yourself as whole, yet it takes practice to actually begin to believe this. However, your thinking and your actions begin to change when this belief actually begins to take effect. Most particularly, you begin to think more universally. *You begin to operate as if the soul is your master.* Since all thought takes form as some level, when you begin to think more universally, your thoughts become more in line with those of the universe and you are more of a beneficial presence to the universe.

In truth, you begin to accept the correct master. As Jesus stated that one cannot serve two masters, there are some hints to correct progression to be in service to the correct master. *The correct master is the soul or God. Otherwise one is in service to the ego.* If one serves the ego, they would tend to be more selfish, self centered and, judgmental.

Remember, *the ego is one's definition of one's self.* If I define myself as a body, then I am defining myself as separate from the whole. Bodies are separate entities as opposed to spirit which is everywhere present. Again, we are to distrust the five senses that tell us of a world of separate things. The purpose of the five senses is to assist you in the world of effects. The five senses do not tell you of the presence of God or the spiritual universe. We are not to place any judgment around this statement about the five senses. They are not bad; they are just doing their job.

However, if one has the correct understanding of the nature of God, one could begin to see that the soul is a better master than the ego. One serves the ego and one serves a more universal master. One is more interested in universal matters and the other is more selfish.

In Eckhart Tolles book *Stillness Speaks*[13] he discusses the ego in a chapter titled "Suffering and the End of Suffering." Here is a portion of that chapter:

> *"What a miserable day."*
> *"He didn't have the decency to return my call."*
> *"She let me down."*

> *Little stories we tell ourselves, often in the form of complaints. They are unconsciously designed to enhance our always deficient sense of self through being "right" and making something or*

someone "wrong." Being "right" places us in a position of imagined superiority and so strengthen our false sense of self, the ego. This also creates some kind of enemy; yes, the ego needs enemies to define its boundary, and even the weather can serve that function.

Through habitual mental judgment and emotional contraction, you have a personalized, reactive relationship to people and events in your life. These are all forms of self-created suffering, but they are not recognized as such because to the ego they are satisfying. The ego enhances itself through reactivity and conflict.

Have you caught this? Ego sees all things as separate and apart from the self. We know of those who consistently complain about things. All you can do is *ask the Holy One to assist you in seeing yourself as one with the all.* You have no ability to do this on your own. Contemplate wholeness in your meditative practice. Invite the Holy One to suggest ways of being aware of self. Do not accept the way you grew up as the way you are to live from this point.

Some years ago I was teaching a Sunday school class at a church I often attended. Somehow the subject of an inner critical voice came up. Three of the children were only four years of age. It was disheartening to hear that children hear that critical voice so early in life. This is the voice of the ego.

Please consider not claiming to have an ego. There is just one ego. You do not own one. Love yourself fully. As a being of spirit, you are love. That is sufficient.

Think about what cancer cells have done. Think about what any diseased cells in your body have done. They have separated themselves from "normal" cells and somehow began to multiply. These diseased cells then do damage to their hosts which is the body.

This is what you do when believing that you are a body. You are separating yourself from the whole. As a separate being, you have no ability to damage the whole of God. You may even do harm to other bodies, but you have no ability to do any damage to the whole of God.

This is a good time to discuss the crucifixion of Jesus. Do you really believe that this really happened as we have been told? Is it possible to kill the son of God? I accept that Jesus was killed, but the Christ nature that this being achieved still lives. This clearly adds to the earlier statement "the eyes lie to us."

The ego may be spoken of as the fall from grace or the dissent into fear. Anytime one falls away from the creator they have fallen into a state of believing that they are separate and must care for themselves. That is a sad situation, but unfortunately that is the primary state of earth right now. Persons on earth are straining to care for themselves.

Since the Holy One is God's answer to this state, it is possible to live under the care of this being and receive its care. Give this a bit of thought. I can either live under the care of God or I can find a way to "make it in this world."

The ego thrives in a state of want. It actually teaches you that having things is the only success. This "wanting, need" is an ego call. Having, being is spirit. The spirit does not know the difference between having and being.

This is what you do when you look at yourself as living under the care of God. You ask for assistance with your life and seek to look at yourself as being under the care of the infinite. You actually become a child of god.

Contemplative Meditation

As part of my spiritual training I spent a great deal of time meditating on wholeness. This means that a part of my meditation practice was devoted to oneness. I suggest that you consider doing the same. To do this you simply say to yourself: "There is only one." You repeat this for about three minutes until you become quiet and listen. Spend the balance of your meditation in the silence. This is called contemplative meditation because you are contemplating oneness.

Now, let's return to the concept of wholeness. Once my mind begins to see itself as whole or define itself as a soul, my objectives change. My thoughts become bigger and my life takes on a new flavor. I have given up the idea of a separate life and see myself as the life of God. God or the soul is my master and miracles become more prevalent in my life. This is because the universe is conscious. The universe knows when one of its members begins to take on a broader picture and the universe responds. One cannot begin to actually direct these miracles, however through prayer one can try. Yet, *one can be faithful to the fact that the universe does not need direction.*

Prayer becomes a time when one communes with their soul. It is not necessarily a time of actually asking for things. However it can be a time of directing ones members. Suppose, for example, one day you sit down with your separate selves and tell them what you are about. All of us having a body are trained to have an ego. Therefore sit down with your ego, your mind, and all of the other concepts that you have of yourself and tell them who they serve. Tell them that from this point forward that all your members are in service to the soul.

This may sound silly. Truly, the ego will not listen, yet this is a start of gathering an understanding of what you are doing and what is taking place. You are listening. Actually, since there are only two possible masters (the ego or God) it is really a simple choice and you are only speaking to these two entities.

These are some of the things that will happen as you progress to be a mind that has started to serve the soul or God:

- Your interest change
- Peace is more prevalent in your makeup (you experience creation's gentleness)
- You ask the soul more often before taking an action on some things
- You love more deeply
- Revelations or ideas of truth come up
- You become more interested in meditation
- You study spiritual principles more through reading and practice
- Laughing or a silliness becomes more common
- Miracles happen (these are not ego directed)
- You gain a habit of saying thank you (God is recognized in all praise)
- Patience grows
- You are more spontaneous (confidently spontaneous)
- The natural abstraction of the mind becomes more prevalent

I am giving you suggestions from personal experience. Your experience of awakening may seem to be different; however there are some common traits. Your experiences are yours. Yet, truth is truth.

Must acknowledge gratitude from this list. Being grateful is like telling the universe that you love it. You cannot grow unless you grow this attitude. Write a list of the things in your life that you are grateful for. Allow a rampage of appreciation to occur within you at times and let this feeling flourish. Consider journaling this "rampage of appreciation."

The changes now are more universal. These changes seem to be personal, yet they are not. Once you begin to see yourself as an aspect of the whole, you simply begin to become God. While God is infinite, the human rising out of form is just that. You rise from being human toward divinity. There is nothing personal about that. There are only judgments or differing views. While your human personality may change, the all is just that. It has no place or specificity. It just is. As you ascend up your spiritual path, the laws do not change. You workload does. Things get appreciably easier.

However, your personal ascension is specific. You may not have reached enlightenment yet, nor has this writer completely. However, the traits of Jesus, the Buddha, and Krishna are similar as are the traits of Mother Teresa, Mahatma Gandhi, and Dr. Martin Luther King who had a wonderful relationship with God. They rose above the ego self and defined themselves as whole. Their actions suggest that they did have a different view of things. These are lives that have been filled with a service attitude, incredible joy, the miraculous, and a feeling of being useful to the creator.

We have the human concept of good attached to these persons. They were altruistic per human definitions. Yet, they had characteristics that suggest a real change had occurred in their mentality. We are not seeking to define what is good. We are simply defining spiritual wholeness, which is a picture of oneself without any confinement. I can love a family, a race, a country or I can love everything. There are essential differences in this definition of love. The suggestion is that the difference is the definition of what you are. Are you willing to begin to define yourself as whole?

When one places too much importance on a physical thing one must be careful. Life is seamless. This is our oneness. Everything is you. You may say that everything is "I." Again oneness is true but can only be practiced and observed to get wonderful benefits. *Love, have confidence, and celebrate the success of everyone as if it were your own.*

I once attended a class where the instructor gave everyone a mirror at the end of the class. The fact is that you are always looking at a mirror. In that spirituality class, the teacher was seeking to subtly teach something about oneness. Everyone is showing yourself to you. The universe is one whole. This is one way I have been taught that God sees things.

Now suppose someone does or says something that angers you. The anger affects you. It can be difficult to listen or notice much from that place of anger. The anger is the ego seeking to cause you to ignore the information the person is showing you so that you do not gain the experience of training yourself how to look at oneness.

Another thing being said here is that it is very beneficial to keep that judging, evaluating voice silent.

Do not compare Mother Teresa and Hitler. These two were mentioned for me to communicate the desire to avoid constant evaluations. Just let them be. Humans have a distinct love of evaluation or judging. Consider an ability to ignore the voice of comparison. For example as part of my own growth, I always hear myself use the word like or dislike. I do not give a lot of thought to this, I just hear myself.

By ceasing evaluations, the ego is silenced. Become an observer of your thoughts and words. The suggestion is to consider the incredible abilities and knowledge of God. Can any human knowledge or learning compare to what God is able to teach you by the willingness to silence your ego. In a way, I am saying that your intelligence is miniscule compared to what God can do through you.

One could consider the power of the silence. This is the ability to just listen within. Out of this quiet and peace, power emerges. Initially this may seem to cause inner disturbances. One must experience this.

Take some time to listen to what comes out of your mouth for periods of time. This is where spiritual practice elevates. Do not judge yourself, just become more conscious.

I had to learn to just meditate each day and often at the end of the day to catch whatever information was being given to me. This is called self observation. Practice meditating at the end of your day which allows you to filter the information that you receive during the day. Some days you benefit from the information, although be careful not to analyze or judge yourself. Observing information is clear, because in your analytical mind everything is judged or is different. Anger or fear must be observed so you can begin to replace them with natural love.

My Holy Self once warned me that I was judging during my meditations. Be conscious about judging yourself. This is not to be a part of your meditation. Just observe without attachment.

The Mind
Now, let's talk about the concept of a split mind which sees separation and operates principally on separation thoughts. A split mind or a lower mind calls itself a body and serves the desires of the ego,

and is not consistent. It principally wants more of the earthly stuff (toys, relationships, money, etc.). Most of life is spent getting or seeking to get and possibly hoarding.

Must admit that this was the way I principally lived. Having these things was to make me happy. Yet, I read repeatedly about how these things do not bring happiness. One can begin to enjoy the principal joy of serving God. That is real joy. That is satisfaction.

Rise above the lower mind that is so ego driven. Call this rising your awakening to desire more awareness of God as your life. Give life to God.

Learn to live within your higher mind. Therefore, you benefit by being directed by the spirit as opposed to your ego. You will always have an ego to deal with. Simply do not be directed by it. Do not fight it or argue with it. You are to free your mind. The Holy Spirit which is also in your mind is your help in this case. Again, I state the desire to tell Holiness of my willingness.

Your Personal Guide

The Holy Spirit has the job of connecting you as a human to your holy state. It does this through healing your split mind that sees itself as separate, because there is just one mind. We can heal quickly when we begin to practice as if there is just one. Actually since all things are ideas that have taken form, begin to share from the idea level and it is easy to see that nothing is lost.

We live in a big fishbowl called mind. Our life experiences show that ideas take form in the mind. Our task is to become aware of what we are thinking. We then begin to learn to let go of any unpleasant thoughts we carry.

For example, you have heard the statement: "I am only human."

Please learn not to make this statement. When you do, you are accepting that your human self is who you are. You are making judgments, limiting ideas, creating fear, and possibly anger. This leads to the inability to rise above these limitations. With the help of the Holy One you rise above all of this while still appearing in a body. You are not limited by the body unless you desire to be.

Love is more than a feeling. Love is both an action word and a noun. In other words we are love in action and we see our love working in places, people, pets and things. It is the recognition of our connection. Through love we recognize our oneness.

On The Contrary

The ego boasts or wants to boast of what it has or complain about what it doesn't have. It is the symbol of separation. It divides itself into countries and supports nationalism, it divides itself into races and supports racism, it divides itself into families by supporting separation and all these examples are temporary alliances. Recognize that these groups have positive attributes. Clearly family has many positives. These alliances break down when something does not go as the ego pleases, and the ego cannot be pleased very long.

When you experience fear, you are listening to the ego. This is choice. All that you see and experience is a result of your choices. You can only learn of this through the Holy One. Remember the trinity.

God, the Son, and the Holy Spirit are the only three real Beings in existence. Everyone experiences an ego and must learn that it is part of the dream. Awaken from this dream and live. If it is not a being in the trinity or a quality that is eternal, it is part of the illusion.

One thing that the ego loves to do is create drama and fights. This is the ego's mode of operation and part of that is divide and conquer. I had an argument with a person that blew up into an unpleasant situation. I understood that the person I argued with appeared to be around a lot of drama and I accepted that I participated in the drama. I later forgave myself for participating and moved on. Affirm your oneness and the oneness of all creation by not participating in drama, stand aside, walk away, or just observe. These you will learn will serve you well. Be aware that the principal ways of dealing with these matters is in consciousness.

An Experience of Depression
There was a time when I was suffering from depression, which is a state of extreme fear and pain. It seemed to come out of nowhere. I wondered where it came from as I was actually having a pret-

ty good life. I learned not to try to figure it out as to source.

Through my study of mysticism, I remember reading about someone who suggested that the spiritual path is a treacherous path. This is because anyone who seeks to fall in love with God is actually on a path of letting separate existence go. What is your separate existence from God?   It is your belief in an ego?

The ego attacks a child of God who simply wants a closer relationship with their creator. In particular, a person once told me that they planned to begin religious studies at church, but were really afraid of what they have seen that spiritual practices can bring. Spiritual practice does not bring pain. You are simply learning to let go of an ego. It is the living in an ego that brings pain. The release of this being is your goal. The benefits are incredible. Remember one of the principles of this book is that guidance by the Holy One is the path to spiritual growth. Seeking to grow with ego guidance is the source of pain.

This is why I believe in the Bible where Jesus states "do not fear, I have overcome the world[11]" Seeking to lead those of us who are seeking spiritual growth, Jesus is saying that he is still here and we must simply call on him. I add that the call to the Holy One is the same call. That is my interpretation of the scripture. In a literal sense, Jesus completed his ascent into the Holy Spirit and is urging us to take the paths that he took toward spiritual mastery.

Jesus the man ascended to the Christ by letting the Holy One become his teacher.

Because you are interested in spiritual growth and you know about the tremendous abilities that Jesus exhibited on earth you can see how valuable the Holy One is. This Being can take you to your height.

Denying Falsities

I had just been advised by my doctor in Los Angeles to take an antidepressant for my bouts of the horrible pains of depression. The drug the Los Angeles doctor prescribed would cause me to become dependent upon it. I felt that I was too young to live on a pill for the rest of my life and most of my life I had been resistant to taking pills. Another friend, an herbalist suggested a collection of herbs for the same thing. Since I knew that herbs do not cause the numerous side effects and are not so addictive, I decided to take the herbs.

A few days later I had a most horrible anxiety attack. The herbs were not helping at all. Yet, there was something within that pain. I was at a crossroad. Though it was painful, that crossroad was good for me. I can learn without pain, but with ego guidance I was not choosing wisely.

When there seems to be no other way, then God is the way.

This statement is a declaration of a belief that you and I have a loving spiritual friend who is right here with us. The power of God is without limit. God's ways are only good and gracious. We must learn to call on this friend and know that this friend will always answer.

If you try to use your mind to figure a way out, you are relying on the ego. You may even begin to look to other beings in the world of form for help. You may feel frustrated that you cannot solve this problem on your own. We therefore go back to that statement in a prior chapter:

If you rely on what you have previously defined as yourself, you will be disappointed.

Turn to Holy One Within

All of us have heard voices within that suggest something as impossible. All of us have the responsibility of becoming aware of ego and learning to tune it out. It is not difficult when the Holy One is remembered. The Holy One is in your mind and it has a voice. Yet its main offering is of peace. Seek to stay in peace and let the Holy One operate in your mind as your real friend and master. This is the type of master that you want. Any feelings of slavery or feeling less than is an ego thought. Do not be resistant to the Holy One.

This willingness to be a servant to the Holy One is simply your declaration of willingness to learn from a perfect and loving teacher. You have become willing to let your mind be cleansed of separation thinking. Most of us have no idea how to do this. Yet the Holy One knows exactly how to do it through you.

1. The first step is the desire for peace. This is the desire for a peaceful mind. Without physically saying things to persons, seek peace with all persons in consciousness as well as a peace with all things and circumstances. Such a mind can hear the Holy One and is willing to obey its messages. It asks very little. Actually you will rarely be asked to do anything.

2. The most difficult request that it will make of you is its request for your stillness which teaches you what you are and how little is asked of you. Its' power is beyond anything you can do. Yet your actions will be directed in such a way that you will not be able to get outside of it. The Holy One and nothing else will direct all actions and nothing but joy will arise.

3. Suppose you are pondering a decision. Simply say: "Holy One, decide for me." You have just given divinity the right to make a

perfect decision for you. Similarly you may jokingly state "It will be fun to see how God deals with this matter" and ask a question on the matter. Then stay in the question and let God answer.

4. Practice this awareness of oneness. Holiness is awaiting your decision to practice the building of this relationship.

5. Patience with the self will grow as well with this practice. Anger thoughts, impatience, and other negative emotions can be common for a person who has been brought up in this world. We heal our world by first healing our own mind.

I was able to heal my experiences of depression through my work with the Holy One. I did not take any medication or herbs to heal it. I became more aware of my wholeness and the sweet gentle being that lives in me. This is the being that is each of us.

Blame

Joyce is a beautician who works in a salon. Her specialty is styling and for a higher price, she also provides hair weaving. She sews hair onto a hair net that is sewn or glued on the hair around the scalp of a client. Joyce makes a good living in this profession. Many of her clients pay her by cash but some pay by check.

One day Joyce brings about $2,000 to work with her intending to make a deposit in the bank that day. Unfortunately she is a little late for work that day and does not go to the bank as a client is waiting for her when she arrives. After finishing that client she has two other clients waiting for her. By the time she gets to the third client she still has not taken a break to go to the bank.

Joyce goes to another area of the salon to check on a client who is getting a shampoo. While Joyce is in this area of the salon, Tina, an assistant of another beautician goes into Joyce's purse and steals the $2,000. When Joyce returned to her station she notices that her purse has been opened, and the money is gone.

"Beatrice, I had money in my purse and I just returned to find that my purse was open. Someone has stolen money from me," Joyce says.

"Is there anyone at your home who you can call to determine if you left your money there," Beatrice responds.

Joyce immediately calls home, hoping that she left the money at home. No one answers the phone at home.

"I must go home now to see if I left my money there."

The money is not anywhere in the house. Now Joyce is getting angry. This amount of money matters to her, and the idea of someone stealing it from her, is quickly putting her in a rage.

Joyce returns to work to try to finish her client's hair and look for her money. But due to the anger rising in her, she can't concentrate on her work. Somehow she manages to complete a few heads, then she just leaves the salon. When she returned home, she goes to her room and starts to cry. She feels so foolish and don't know what she should do next.

After a difficult night's sleep Joyce returns to the salon the next day. An hour later she notices that Tina goes out to lunch and returns with a new purse.

"Are you that same person who is always complaining that you do not have enough money? I see you have a new purse," says Joyce.

"That is really none of your business. I wanted a nice purse. I now have one," Tina responds.

"Nice my ass. You are the one who stole money from me."

"I haven't stolen anything."

"Beatrice, this is the one who stole my money."

"Joyce, do you have any proof that Tina stole your money"

"All I know is that she is suddenly acting very rich and this is the same person who is usually complaining about not having money," says Joyce.

"Why don't the two you just go back to work and try to stay apart for the rest of the day," Beatrice suggests.

"I can't take this. I am going home," Joyce says as she walks out of the salon.

Still so infused with anger, directed at Tina, Joyce cancels appointments for the next day so that she can stay at home. While at home Joyce just cries and talks constantly over the phone with her mother. Her mother lives in a distant city. She called her father, Victor.

"Dad, someone stole some money from me at work and I cannot work there anymore having to see that person each day," Joyce says while crying.

"Sometimes things just happen that we can do nothing about. Things have a way of surfacing sometimes and they cannot always be dealt with directly. Somehow you need to release that anger," Victor responds.

"I want my money or Tina needs a good lesson."

"Please don't do anything rash," says her father.

Joyce decides to call Beatrice to talk to her about the situation.

"Beatrice, I am so angry that I cannot work there with Tina."

"Joyce, you do have a client load that you are not serving and you will miss any walk in potential money if you stay at home," says Beatrice.

Tina was hired by Beatrice to shampoo and monitor the ladies who are under the hair dryer. Beatrice also notices that Tina is strangely abundant with her spending of late.

After a few days of Tina's errant behavior and Joyce not returning to work, Beatrice, the owner of the salon decides to fire Tina. When Beatrice told Joyce, she said "there was another incident with Tina at the salon, she's gone and I need you to return to work. Joyce returns to work and begins once again serving her clients with their hair care needs.

Some week's later Joyce's father Victor is in the salon getting a haircut. There is one male barber in this salon that does very good haircuts.

"That situation with Joyce's money being stolen brought a lot of heat to this work situation for awhile," says the barber.

"Did others in the salon know about the situation?" Victor asked.

"Everyone seemed to know. Most were expecting Joyce to do something about it."

"Well, there was little Joyce could do about it," Victor comments.

"Joyce deserves a medal for not doing anything. She had no proof, but it was obvious to most that Tina was guilty. I know I would have done something. Tina might have found her tires suddenly flat if it had happened to me," this barber then stated.

While it is recognized that Tina did steal the money, Joyce did nothing. This writing suggests a different way of looking at this incident. In spite of her anger, she is to be complimented for not taking the advice of other immature minds that believe that a person has the right to punish another.

Let's take a moment to focus on the Victor's comments. Maybe it was not said with appropriate compassion, but we cannot always understand why things happen unless we understand the mechanics of the ego.

Regardless of the fact that there was no justice rendered to Joyce in by getting her money back. Joyce can grow if she begins to accept that she and the ego created this situation.

Joyce created all the characters in this story within her mind. It is the result of a split mind. A mind that tends to place blame and then somehow feels that anger is justified, which only creates more damage. This is no judgment on the value of Joyce, nor should anyone say that she deserved Tina stealing from her. We learn by seeing how ego gathers its members to create havoc. Who knows how much worse this matter could have been if Joyce had chosen to seek to inflict some punishment on

Tina as some of her co-workers had suggested. Fortunately this did not happen. Inflicting punishment may please the ego for a moment. As a child of God with the awareness of oneness, why inflict harm on anyone?

Defining Moments Lead to The Holy One

Throughout life each of us experience times of extreme emotional pain. These times are defining moments for us. Depression was mine. They are necessary for growth and movement into spiritual maturity. Extreme emotional pain is the only reason some seek out God. It sometimes takes a place of exhaustion and being totally without a solution for some of us to begin that road to God while in a body. We certainly do not wish to await life's seeming end to get to God. We can start this process without extreme pain if we choose. The Holy One is the only avenue to real spiritual growth, leading to maturity.

It is not our place to understand why things happen. It is our place to learn to let the physical world go at times. Let things be. We begin to believe that there is a natural justice that governs all things. For this reason we do not try to figure out why this happened to Joyce. Her place is to learn to let the universe govern itself. It does govern itself. It has a natural way of doing things and through our willingness to just let God be God, we learn of its power.

The ego states of fear and anger are opposite states to love and peace. The purpose of the story about Joyce is to learn that when in anger about something, we have let the ego dominate our existence. The opposite of this is to let our spirit dominate our existence. Of course Joyce was hurt personally and financially by what occurred. Yet, she must choose how she is to move through this experience. The Holy One is the comforter. Its peace is the comfort.

God does not defend or attack anyone or anything. Neither should you or I. There is no benefit in hurting myself. The universe has a beautiful mechanism for this.

Personal Health

From what you have read so far about the ego now it is time to begin understanding that the ego is your primary producer of disease and pain. Joyce's story suggests that it is a producer of extreme anger and viciousness. A personal but, simple story will suffice here.

I was sitting in a park studying my first book with a group. Several friends had asked that I go through this book of spiritual practices with them. I was happy to oblige. We were covering one chapter each week.

One of the participants noted that I took several breaks to go to the restroom during one of our meetings.

"It is normal as we get older that we must take these potty breaks often," she said.

I just looked at her and smiled. I also noted a feeling within me.

Later that evening during my meditation I was told from within that the potty breaks happen quite often when I am in a judgmental state of mind. I did not know I was judging anyone, so I paid attention to what it said. It also seemed to happen when I got excited. Now I have healed this condition through placing attention elsewhere.

I had seen a commercial on television for a pill that supposedly helps a person with frequent urination. It also talked about the possible side effects of the meditation. Now suppose someone takes the pill for this condition and have dealt with the situation from the level of the body and may get some relief. However, they have ignored or are not aware of the root of their condition which is the ego thought. They are dealing with the condition from the level of the body. They have not done anything to change their thoughts which continue to damage the body. The pill may deal with the problem of frequent urination while the body continues to be damaged by ego thoughts. This is why so many of our elder citizens have a pill regimen as a part of their day. Often one pill is to deal with the side effects of one of the other pills.

Albert Einstein is famous for his statement that "problems cannot be dealt with at the level of the problem." He also said, "One must rise above the level of the problem."

I say *again*, "each of us is a spiritual being." You deal with your health from your understanding of what you are. Deal with things in your spirit more often and you gain a greater opportunity to deal from the proper perspective.

This means to set your understanding of what you are as a whole being made of love. Love cannot get sick. I also understand that if sickness does occur, I do not critique myself. I do the mental work as a priority and whatever is necessary to express love of that body.

The body is neutral. The mind takes on the sickness and projects the sickness into the body. As you clean up your mind, good health is one of the wonderful benefits. There may still be times when you have to take a pill, see a doctor, or use other means to heal your body. However when you elevate your mind, the benefits are limitless.

Explain Illness, shall we?

In our world, the medical and scientific communities are investing tremendous amounts of money and time researching ways to cure all kinds of diseases. However the mind is projecting sickness into the body, we are drugging or cutting parts of our bodies in an attempt to heal it. From this simple statement about the mind, you begin to see the possibilities of how you can aid in the healing of your body. The medical community has made some gains and creating cures, but these gains will not heal our minds, while the ego is creating more disease.

Please take a moment to consider the enormity of these simple statements. You may think that these simple statements are *too* simple to provide the enormous benefits that they suggest. Well, God's lessons are always simple. Only the ego desires and pushes complexity.

What about when a baby becomes ill? Are they innocent? Can they attract disease? A human birth is not a new life. Life is eternal and continuous. There really are no births or deaths. Do not try to figure out the physical! You learn and grow as you begin to let the inner knower take care of things. Assume your proper place.

Your spiritual nature is innocent. As your spiritual nature grows within consciousness, so does your awareness of your innocence. Your spiritual nature is the truth about you. This is saying something to you about the ego use of guilt. Accept this as truth.

You are not here to figure out the physical world. . Appreciate the progression of science as you learn how to live with God and the world of spirit which is the cure for all manifestation of illness. Several times a day, put your mind on the Holy One and experience good health and wholeness.

The Bible speaks of *unceasing prayer*. My belief is that Jesus and Buddha as well as the large numbers of persons who have spiritually ascended to high levels have *learned to put their egos aside*. The degree to which they did this is tells of the level of their spiritual growth. Such a thing as growth cannot be measured nor shall I make an attempt. Essentially, you must prove to yourself that you are not an ego. You are a limitless being of spirit gifted with unlimited power through grace.

Learning to Distrust God
Placing blame is without merit. God is everywhere. The ego attempts to teach one to distrust God. Having spent many years on the prayer line at church, I have spoken too many who really distrust God. Truthfully, I did at one time wonder where God was in my life. Many of us have had to learn to

trust God. Sometimes it takes spiritual courage to learn this lesson.

Remember the ego can be a belief of who I am. When I only go by what I see and my past experiences, spiritual growth cannot happen—perhaps this is called the "victim mentality." Spiritual growth requires a belief in the unseen. Sounds like the definition of faith coming through for those of you who know the definition of faith. *Faith is a belief in the unseen.*

God did not create ego and God did not create a devil. Physical forms are temporal and most are neutral. All that is eternal is real creation. Nothing created by God can be destroyed. As we grow more fully into God by studying God, we have the experience of knowing that this erroneous being called ego does not exist. A God of love does not create pain for itself. I am this "itself."

There really is no one to blame. Forgive. *Forgive yourself for listening to the ego. Forgive yourself for not listening to God.* My experiences are a result of what I think. My thoughts and beliefs simply return to me. This is why the love of all creation becomes my dominant thought.

There is no value in learning to distrust God. If we begin to accept many of our worldly experiences as illusion the opposite occurs. God is really loved by us. Much that we see and use to place blame is a block that we have set up between God and ourselves. There is a natural love that each of us has for God. Removing this block opens the way for this love to come through.

I have a friend who like me, facilitates spiritual training workshops and personal counseling sessions in Los Angeles. He said the following to me:

"I like and am aware of what you do, but I don't understand how you deal with all the crying and suffering that clients bring to you. I love to speak with people, but I can't deal very well with the crying, wailing and personal suffering."

"I do not get caught up in their pain. If I do, it impedes my ability to heal them." I answered.

I have learned at times to keep the Holiness of my clients on the prayer line and in my private counseling sessions in my mind in spite of what they say. I learned much of this through praying with people who call the prayer line.

I listen to a great deal of the pain, and I endure their suffering words, yet it has become clear to me that this endurance is necessary to assist. On the prayer line, I do not counsel as this requires too much speaking and unfortunately it can turn into my starting to analyze the mind of my clients. *Analysis is not an answer.*

My desire is to be aware of the Holiness of those on the phone and those who visit me in person. I look past what my eyes, ears, and any of my senses are saying. The truth is still true. Holiness is everywhere. The body's eyes do not see this nor do the body's ears hear it. I turn away from the bodily senses and let my holy mind do the work. This is healing. This is what I do.

The Human Mind Does not Heal

I cannot let my human mind direct these processes. It cannot heal, nor does it understand. My humanness is required to observe and let the power within do that which it desires to do. This love force loves to love. I am just willing to join in by loving and I do not let my littleness get in the way of these healings. These forces know exactly what to do. They are at work while my humanness just observes.

God can absolutely be trusted. One cannot grow spiritually unless one begins to trust God who answers all your questions and bring you the peace of God so that you can live a life worth living. You cannot live an ego directed life. This is a life of consistent pain and suffering. This is why so many believe that life is a struggle.

There is only one struggle in life. That is your struggle to learn what is true and what is not. All truth is eternal and true. This means that the truth does not change from time to time or change with the seasons. For this reason the Holy One when dealing with your beliefs must work with diligence because your power is the same as that of Holiness. The difference is that Holiness cannot become confused.

Life is Good

Is life good? Consider this question and decide whether you are to enjoy life or not. When the ego takes you hostage it is because you are being too incensed about occurrences that happen in the physical world, you become its slave. Your freedom has been taken. Who wants that? This ego is a voice that you have created in your mind and this is not a voice you are to follow. It is cunning, but will create a living hell for you here on earth if you follow it. God did not create an ego for you and you must prove to yourself that you are now love and nothing else. Seek to live in love and peace with everyone and everything and a different life becomes available to you.

Jesus in The Sermon on the Mount suggested that we pluck out the eyes and cut off the ears if necessary. Of course, he did not mean this literally. He was speaking of the distrust of the senses. You learn not to attach meaning to that which you can see.

Practice this exercise with your eyes.

Begin your day looking at things around you. Tell yourself that none of these things mean anything. As you go through your day, keep your awareness up and avoid attaching meaning to what you see. God created a meaningful world. That world you can begin to experience. It is one that is absolutely enjoyable.

Suppose, for example, that someone does something in front of you that you do not appreciate and you say that the person is mean. Avoid putting meaning on something that you observed. Yes, it happened. Yes, you did not like it, but it does not mean anything. Label no one as mean. Remember, God is all that exists.

Bad Neighborhoods Are Mind Judgments
Say you have to walk through a bad neighborhood. Do you really want to judge a neighborhood in that way? You created it in your mind. Create beauty by believing that beauty is all that exists and there is the doorway to a living heaven.

I had an experience in my mind of changing the belief that I was living in a bad neighborhood some years ago. After some arguments and a few unpleasant experiences I decided to change my mind about the community I lived in. I eliminated the thought in my mind that it was a bad neighborhood. As a morning and evening walker, I had to walk through a community that might by crime statistics be called a bad neighborhood.

I began a process that I now call healing my mind of the erroneous thought about that neighborhood. My changes made contributions to people in that community, however I didn't believe that my changes would change the crime statistics in that community. People began to respect and care for me and I can attest to the fact that many were affected by my contributions. God is just so able. I am just a willing servant.

In reality I had no choice. I love to walk and find it a pleasant part of my lifestyle. Only in hindsight can I say that the results were incredible. Join me and Holiness in healing your mind. One cannot begin to understand the light ahead as the mind heals. Each day is such a joy.

Learn that experience is a poor teacher. As your mind heals, your experiences will change. A healed mind has forgiven the world. Walk through the world you have forgiven. Let it be. Another world has opened up to you. Live there.

Another aspect of the ego is that it seems to always be looking for opportunities to be unhappy. Consider your mind is a beautiful light and the ego creating clouds to hide or obscure the light. In order to reach and experience the peace of that light one has to clear up the clouds.

I cannot allow my thoughts about any form cause me to believe that God has lost its purity. Whether a whorehouse or a church, I must at least be willing to believe that the omnipresence of God is true and that the light is always shining. I only have judgments about things that cause me to form conscious or unconscious opinions. These judgments cause me to believe that certain places or situation are good or bad.

This may be a little difficult to accept, but wherever I am and wherever you are God is. My ability to operate as a Christ presence is dependent upon my ability to hold to these truths regardless of situation or circumstance.

A Simple Example

I am standing in a long line at a grocery store. Another patron of the store is standing in line behind me.

"The manager of this store needs to do something about this line. I am so frustrated with this situation, I could scream," says the person behind me.

"Yeah, it would be easy for another checker to open up another line at one of those empty cash registers. Maybe a few people didn't come to work today at this store. I have better things to do than stand in this like all day," I respond.

"This is the last time I will ever come in this store. This situation is a mess. I too have better things to do," this person then says.

Anger, frustration and impatience are mental qualities that muddle the pool of one's mind. I have seen old western movies where an angry crowd decides to lynch a person as a group of minds stir up anger and, frustration, and possibly impatience with the legal system in place at the time.

Now suppose I am in my right mind (God or some quality of God is on my mind or I had a wonderful mediation experience that morning). I find myself in the same situation at a grocery store in a lengthy line.

"The manager of this store needs to do something about this line. I am so frustrated with this situation, I could scream," says the person behind me.

With a light smile, I acknowledge that the person has said something to me.

"Don't you think the store should do something about this situation?" There are several cash registers here where they could easily open another line," the person adds further.

"It would be good if another checker came to speed up this line," I add with a light smile acknowledging the statements made to me.

Each person has a choice of how they are to view each moment of their lives. Living in a state of peace is certainly preferable to a state of impatience and frustration. One of the purposes of this book is to assist the reader in learning to live in a state of peace. Knowing that Jesus was at times referred to as the "prince of peace" brings up one of my beliefs about the Christ Mind. I believe that the Christ Mind is in a perpetual state of peace in spite of situations or circumstances.

The Christ Mind is within each of us. It is available to us. We can learn to take control of our emotions and attitudes, however having access to this mind means much more. This is the mind within that performs miracles.

God is present in all things. Unfortunately there are ideas, attitudes, and conditioning that I am unaware of. These states of mind are really clouds that block the light of God's love and power to operate in our life and experiences.

Everyone has met someone who has had a bad experience and has become fearful of it happening again.

"I will never do that again or I will never allow that to happen to me again."

Psychology calls this paranoia. This is living in fear that I once experienced with depression. Personal mind training is what allowed me to grow through that horrible experience. I now consider that experience of depression a real blessing. Of course, I would never want to relive such an experience, but admittedly it gave me the resolve to do my mental work. I simply wanted to live a better life and began to believe that it was my mind that needed healing.

For that reason, I have found it helpful to honestly claim Christhood as my real nature. It is what I am. It is what everyone and everything is.

Christhood is simply a quiet confidence and assurance that I live in God. It is necessary that I practice this belief as I go through my day. This means that I begin to see or believe that I live in a fishbowl filled with the love of my creator. Everything I see and all things are actually seeking to tell me this, but I must not let my clouds block my vision. While one could believe that the clouds are normal in life, but this contrast with the statement that God is all there is.

Having done much work to change my mind I can testify to the power of God that is in all. The process is sometimes called mind purification. An earlier chapter suggested the strength of the belief that love is everywhere. Improper personal beliefs and attitudes are the blocks that can keep me from experiencing the power that I am.

Everyone is the light of the world. I have chosen to allow my light to grow by doing mental exercises that clear up the mental dramas or clouds that can and do block the light from shining through. This is a light that cannot be seen with eyes, but it is simply the light of God's love within all.

A Natural Love

Forgiveness is a powerful spiritual practice. If the three dimensional world that we live in is an illusion and we learn to forgive, love remains. Remove anything that is not godly. Now you can experience the natural love you have for your creator and the natural love your creator has for you.

This natural love is heaven or the Kingdom of Heaven and it is the place where spirits live, and all things are one. It is a blissful experience that can be experienced more often. Here you are unified with God. Yes, it usually is a very different way of living. Yet as you are a wonderful being of love, let love dominate your experience without knowing what it is. Learn to just let things be. What you need to know will come to you.

There is another path, where I learn to think differently.

To understand this natural love, look at the limited human concept of love.

Human love is often a trade of affection for affection. This trading concept is unnatural. Our concept of an economy is based upon trading. Yet, love must not be one of those things that go so often on the auction block. Many get hurt deeply by this type of love because it is unnatural. These are usually just attachments.

It is the common ego that joins people together temporarily as an alliance. It is really an agreement to get something from another. We see this sometimes called patriotism, family, friends, companies, and joint ventures. Ego is in a constant state of need. Love is what you are and these alliances are a part of our society.

Most countries of our planet are economic systems built for the benefit of the citizens. We have divided our world based upon citizenships and cultural differences. Please learn to have them and understand their purpose.

Our spiritual and intellectual maturity now allows us to live among others more easily if we can leave our ego in check. With that in check, the process of living gracefully is improved.

The choice to love someone or something is often a desire to experience of what you already have. You were made out of love. Do you need anyone to tell you that they love you in order to know that you are lovable? This answer is obvious since you are made of love.

There is nothing wrong with loving another person. Romance and sex novels sell because we enjoy this experience. There are parts of us that cannot distinguish between reality and fiction.

Remember: Thoughts take form.

Yet these human love experiences do not teach natural love. God loves all things equally. There is no special love or compartmental affection in God. This equanimity of love is a challenge in the physical world.

We do not need to figure out the physical world since our eyes do not tell us the whole truth. Nothing ever dies in the spirit world and everything lives under natural love. Animals operate under an instinctual survival mechanism. Humans also have survival instincts. However, being willing to work hard for something that we already have is questionable.

Restating a God Created Being

It is appropriate to restate a God Created Being. God creation is eternal. Humans do not live forever. The spirit in humans is what God created. The human can contain an ego which creates havoc at times. What God has created has no ability to create havoc.

Natural love really is not often experienced in the physical world because it is spiritual. We get close, yet the physical world limits it. Natural love has no conditions. No trading. If you are in any relationship with someone, allow the Holy Spirit in to bless it. Only one partner needs to do this. The Holy One will bring the other one along when one partner takes on this task. Although you are in this world, doing this has the ability to bring your relationships up a few notches.

Pray to the Holy One and in your prayer tell the Holy One that this relationship exists for the purposes that the Holy One has given it. Consider your previous reason for the relationship.

Here you learn that you do not enter relationships for sex, money or appearance. You may do that, but wake up and turn the relationship over to the Holy One. Then it becomes a relationship that you treasure. You then get to experience the seamless space of heaven.

Yet it is necessary to understand what the mind is composed of and what it is capable of. I can create an ego in my mind and it can and will create chaos if I am not careful. Perseverance in thought and action is necessary for growth. It is my hope that each gain a greater awareness and understanding of how the ego performs.

Consider making this your last study of ego. It was done for you to know your choices more clearly. You cannot serve two masters, nor should you continually study both.

Healing

Healing of disease is under the same laws. It is simply the mind becoming aware of truth. We eject ego thoughts and the body heals. Heal the mind and the body follows. Learn that only the creations of God are real and you have started down the right path. What has no cause has no effects. Learn what this statement means. Illness is not a creation of God. It has no cause and therefore does not exist. This is the healing that is necessary.

Do learn to age graciously. The body will age and this must not be taken as bad. It simply is a fact of the physical system. Do not resist the aging process.

I once heard a person say that one get uglier as they age. One may need to look at what beauty is. It certainly is not physical.

Enjoy aging as part of your journey. Do accept that proper thinking does slow the aging process. Once again joy is reparative. The Holy One is the source of this joy.

An ego is always in want and is sometimes straining to get. This is unhealthy. The stress of living this way is so painful and can be a cause of illness. Imagine if you allowed someone to make you angry, and you carry this anger for a long time. Can you see how anger must be creating something? This is another reason why forgiveness is so important. You know when you have an experience of truth because it is an experience of God and it is incredible.

Suppose a doctor told you that you are diabetic. Is this really what you are? These labels when accepted become harder to lose. You can experience symptoms of such things, but never accept these things as your truth. Deny the labels by becoming whole in mind. Learn the power of turning away from untruths.

You are not becoming impractical; you are becoming more capable of dealing with life. A person can learn to heal themselves by denying falsities.

Never forget that a logical mind may suggest that some old beliefs are "natural." It may then be assumed that some things suggested here are unnatural. Each is absolutely dependent upon Holiness to assist in strengthening their belief system. It is the pleasure of Holiness to assist here. In fact, only Holiness can really strengthen your beliefs with your willingness. Remember your willingness is critical here. Tell Holiness of your willingness to grow faith.

Practice forgiveness by saying, "I forgive myself." That is all that is necessary. Learn to forgive your unholy ego thoughts. Forgive yourself for forgetting that you are pure spirit.

Backing Up
I have a process that I call "back up." At times I back away from what I might do as a body and I

step away or back away and just observe. I become quiet, aware of what is going through my mind, body as well as my surroundings. I let the spirit present itself and I attempt to become a better listener.

The purpose of this is to remind myself that I am a spiritual being. I take some "body" out of my life because I am so much more than a body.

We are learning the way to health and joy is the Holy One sharing soul satisfying thoughts of joy with us. These thoughts can be brought to us in books or through things we find in other mediums. Inner joy is the cure for all disease which maintains and sustains us. My attitude determines my altitude.

It is quite common in this world for people to place so much faith in the physical. Such things as having a healthy diet and exercising regularly are the physical things we are often taught to place so much emphasis upon.

Having a good diet and exercising the physical body are important to physical health. Yet they are secondary to releasing the ego. With a perfect diet and consistent exercise one can still experience a very unhealthy and unhappy life if they carry ego thoughts which are fear and anger based. These will kill a body.

Please listen carefully: All negativity is impersonal. We learn to separate act from actor by not claiming that people are devilish. All are children of God. You cannot grow spiritually until you learn this. All the seams in your mind are healing. Judgments are passing away.

In any situation where you see someone that causes you to think of negativity, remember the Christ within that person. Let the truth be so.

Since all is one, you grow by letting the truth be true for all. Did you get it? There is only one mind. We are to clear that mind by turning away from error. We are not to claim that it is over there in that person. This will accomplish nothing.

There are persons doing unpleasant things in the world. Yet it is not our place to see evil or error within these persons. This does not accomplish anything. If you want to clear your mind, you see things and take a breath. You let them go. This does not mean that you may never on occasion say something nor do something about what is happening. The most important thing you can do for yourself is to at times tell yourself that error does not exist.

God is all there is.

All the great mystics believe this, and they are helping us to clear our minds of otherness so that God can be there. This takes practice and desire. Yes, you can do it.

Clear your holy mind and let natural love show you what real love is. All of creation is infused with this natural love and it binds the universe together. There is no pain in this love. Even if a love relationship ends, understand that perhaps it relied too greatly upon the physical. It may have been affection with strong attachment. Love never creates pain. Let the Holy One teach you how to truly love and that will be a love you will treasure.

CHAPTER NINE

The Top of the Food Chain

I had the pleasure of visiting Sea World in San Diego, California some years ago. Sea World is a theme park where sea animals are exhibited for entertainment. It was a beautiful, sunny and warm day. There is one sea animal that is at the top of the food chain of the sea. This is an intelligent mammal with a sonar system that allows it to dominate the sea.

Most of us have read how dangerous sharks are. A shark has several lines of teeth on the top and bottom of their jaws. These teeth can rip a hole in anything if given a chance. Sharks also have ability to sense blood in the water and they have feelers like antennae that allow them to move through dark areas of the deep sea and operate without difficulty.

Yet the top of the food chain of the sea is the killer whale. Intelligent, powerful, and skillful they are excellent entertainers at Sea World. Their trainers are dressed in waterproof outfits as they are constantly in and out of the water. These trainers spend a lot of time working with the killer whales during their performances.

My wife and children began a conversation about what most of the trainers of these animals have degrees in.

"I wonder what kind of training those trainers have," Shae said.

"Maybe they are trained in marine biology or something like that," I responded.

"I don't know what marine biology is, all I know is that they have to be very brave to get into the water with those killer whales," Kenya stated.

"Maybe when we get a chance we should ask one of the trainers what they are trained in," said Van.

After the killer whale show we did have a chance to have a brief conversation with one of the killer whale trainers.

"What are most of your trainers of the killer whales trained in?" Van asked.

"Most of our trainers have degrees in some area of behavior studies," the trainer responded.

"That makes sense. You would want to understand what motivates those animals to keep yourselves safe," I remarked.

I once read about an elephant in a circus that killed her trainer because this trainer used cruel methods to train the elephant. That elephant stepped on her killing her.

This tells me that animal trainers have to have more than simple methods in animal training for their own safety. Because they trained and studied the animal's behavior, they are able to survive while using the animals.

A killer whale can weigh up to 12,000 pounds, range in length from 23 to 32 feet, lives from 50 to 60 years, and is a carnivore. Being a carnivore means that the animal eats other animals. Killer whales also have an ability to make sounds in the water and like bats have sonar that tells them of the other things in the water when they read their sonar. They read their sonar by interpreting the vibrations that return to them.

Killer whales hunt in pods that can be large in size. Can you imagine how much these animals in a pod of twenty must eat to maintain their total weight of 240,000 pounds? This number is the weight of 20 killer whales that weigh 12,000 pounds each. These pods can contain up to 40 killer whales and through distinctive sounds that the members of the pod make they communicate over long distances with other members of the pod. These sounds enable group hunting and schemes that read like government intelligence reports.

The killer whales eat fish, birds, whales, squid, and are able to snatch animals off floating ice such as walruses. Due to their intelligence, their enormous appetites, physical power, and their skilled hunting tools (sonar sounds) and methods they have earned their titles as the top of the food chain of the sea. There is nothing in the sea that threatens them in their pods.

Now, as for a trainer, getting in the water with one of these animals how does this trainer manage them? You certainly wouldn't use any electrical prods. Perhaps you show them affection and study their behavior based upon caressing and feeding them.

The Animal that Dominates Earth
The human being is physically a very weak and frail being. Yet this being dominates the earth. The human is at the top of the food chain on planet earth because of his intelligence. This intelligence causes the human to be the most adaptable being on the planet. We can live in extreme cold, tropics and desert regions where lack of water is where so little life exists. Water is the primary need of all life as we understand life to be. The fact that the human

can adapt to desert environments says something about the adaptability of this being.

Our intelligence is part of our spiritual power. That power is amplified under proper direction. All animals have intelligence. As was mentioned previously, all animals also have a connection to God through their intuitive faculties, yet the human has something additional. The Holy One is available to the human. A human may become conscious of this. Knowledge is valuable; combining it with your intuitive faculties is real power.

At the top, nothing threatens the existence of life as a species. For example a lion can kill a human, but lions do not threaten the existence of human life. Mankind across the planet is threatening many animal habitats. Humans are destroying the rainforest which supplies much of the oxygen to the planet. Plants give off oxygen while humans provide plants carbon dioxide. This is the trade that we make with plants.

Many plants are under the sea and these plants are supplying oxygen to the earth system. Humans have not begun much expansion to undersea environments. We are not doing as much damage to the undersea plants. These plants still supply oxygen to the sea that eventually rises above the sea.

One of my teachers once remarked that the aboriginal tribes of Australia have lived on the earth for over 5,000 years. They have done this without any traceable damage to their environment. We can say this about most native indigenous tribes of planet earth. They seemed to live in harmony with their environment without damaging it. With mankind being at the top of the food chain, we must begin to replicate the good habit of living in harmony with our environment.

Global warming is just one of the symptoms that tell us of the potential damage that humans are inflicting on the environment. It is believed by some that the preponderance of hurricanes in past years is a result of global warming. Here we are using the illusion to guess at the cause of other conditions in an illusion. While it is known that there can be many human created conditions that may be the cause of global warming, we cannot be sure.

As we gain the habit of believing that inner conditions cause all outer conditions. Looking at the outer, thoughts and beliefs are true causes of outer conditions.

Having spent some time in the world of finance and economics, I understand that the US economy is a very complex one that feeds off of economic activity to generate spending. We study supply and demand. We study money creation in the banking system. We study government spending. We also study taxing policies by various government agencies to try to keep the economy moving. In spite of these physical factors economist have come up with a term called consumer confidence to try to measure the effect of mind on the economy. If consumers are not financially confident they spend less. If they begin to spend less the economy suffers. We need not forget the power of the mind in our lives.

The study of consumer confidence is an attempt at looking at an inner cause to suggest an outer effect. The inner mental state is the confidence of a mass of people. The outer is the economic strength of the economy. This tells me that large numbers of people are beginning to study mental factors as a cause of a very important area of our lives. Since mind is God, we can say that economists are beginning to study God to help determine the direction of our economy.

Advertisers spend big money to get their products in movies and in parts of television shows. For example, car makers pay movie makers to use their cars in movies. The same takes place on television shows when the car is used on the show.

Television is selling you the world of illusion. These advertisers seek to invoke some emotional response to bring the audience into the commercial. Too much television can be a cause for you to believe what you see on television as truth which impedes spiritual growth. This world is often in direct opposition to the world of spirit. Spiritual growth requires a growing in belief of that you cannot see as well as some reliance on the five senses. If you live in a way that you are constantly using your five senses in heightened awareness, you can expect that your reliance in the spiritual sense is lessened.

There is nothing wrong with allowing television to entertain you. However you must be spiritually strong enough to do this. You are learning to live in truth. This means that you are not so easily swayed be what you see.

In this chapter we talked about the progress of animal trainers who are now studying the minds of the animals. They still use outer means to stimulate the animals, yet their study is behavioral. . Remember, mind is God. The study of mind whether it is in an animal or a human is the study of God.

The purification of mind is the cleansing of erroneous thought. Recall that the Holy One has the responsibility of assisting our spiritual growth. Studying behavior and using our beliefs are the primary way we study mind. Without it we just look at outer conditions. Beliefs are the primary things that drive the mind. These animals perform because they have come to associate a particular behavior with receiving food from their trainers. Each of us operates within a world of what we believe. Just imagine if more of us began to believe that Holiness was everywhere. This is a personal decision.

Dropping Beliefs about God

Many of our beliefs about God are erroneous. The purification process of the mind is about dropping these beliefs. In this way the truth presents itself clearly. God is truth. When we look at the dominant figures of the planet, we are using our five senses. These are the tools of the ego. Learning to drop these tools is like the ego dying.

When the ego is diminished, true life is given greater opportunity to come forth. Our actual ability to see improves. This is true vision where the heart begins to see through our eyes... *We actually begin to see Holiness everywhere. The Christ is rising from the tomb and a personal Easter time is taking place.* As you begin your march toward Holiness, these experiences become common. Initially they are like dreams so brief that you may doubt that they even happened.

Your life is changing and when you begin to remember these dreams, they are important to you. They speak of a life very different from the one that you are accustomed to. You begin to look at yourself differently. On one occasion I recall a dream where I was somehow with God. In this dream it was as if I was a voice as was God because I saw nothing. Then God told me to look in a direction. As I gazed in the direction, I saw something so magnificent that I said "What have you done! What have you done?"For some reason I was terribly excited and began crying tears of joy.

I understand that this is what God sees when he looks at his child. What I saw cannot be described. In complete awe I believe it was a way of looking at the Kingdom of Heaven. I cannot honestly recall what I saw. Yet, I maintain that I was looking straight at the Kingdom. The cosmic cannot be confined completely with words. A Santa Clause God may be good to a point; yet living as this being part of me is a bit different.

Dreams

At one time I was not aware of my dreams. I simply slept so deeply that I rarely recalled them. However, one day I decided to journal something that had come to me in a dream. It must be understood that many dreams are symbolic. There is an easy key to this symbolism. You must consult with the Holy One about communications through dreams. This is the only sure way to understand this symbolism.

Keep your visions to yourself. Letting them out too quickly is like giving your pearls to swine. You can lose any growth and begin to doubt what you experience by talking to others who do not share your heightened state.

Certainly, the act of staying in the company of those who also consider themselves on the spiritual path is a good thing. This can be called spiritual community or fellowship. Otherwise, it is easy to feel pulled away from truth. You are what God made and nothing else. Sharing this in classes or study groups is awesome. Choose your path, beautiful one. The path to God is wondrous.

There may come a time when you take on a task too big for your mind. This gives an opportunity to practice sharing something magnificent. For God is magnificent. You practice creating with God to bring forth something you can only imagine. Imagine!

You share the will of God without being fully aware of what makes you faithfully say yes to that will. The nature of God is magnificence. Therefore knowing that these symbolic dreams have meaning and purpose, you can seek to become aware of their meaning without loss or fear. Just enjoy them.

In this way the judging mind is losing power. A fully open heart is compassionate and agrees only with the gracious ways is what you want.

All of mankind must begin to understand the mind and begin to purify it if we want to continue to enjoy prosperous lives and live together in harmony. However, each of us must take a personal responsibility in this purification process and the spread across the world will become obvious. Through purification we let go of human beliefs and allow the thoughts of God to dominate our existence.

CHAPTER TEN

A Natural Way

It is natural to be in constant communication with the creator. Humans have taught themselves the unnatural way of not being in constant communication with the creator. Certainly there was a time when I thought God was hard to contact. This is because I believed that I had to do something like meditation, or prayer to be with God. Fortunately my beliefs have changed.

There are several ways to be in contact with the creator. There are also several ways to be in constant contact with the creator:

- Verbal prayer when you are alone and talking or writing to God.

- Non-verbal prayer where one is speaking with God in thought.
- Formal meditation where one is still.
- Living in the now (this is the natural way)

Verbal Prayer, the Act of Praise

In this state a person is speaking aloud to God, or through their writing or some other physical manner like dancing. For example, I often write letters to God. These letters may be requests for something or they are letters thanking God for some area of my experience. While on this topic, it is suggested that you consider this method of communication. Writing letters of gratitude to God is very healthy. It actually raises one's vibration.

When you praise God it is a feeling of great love for God. God is not responding because reality is a seamless space. Praising God is a praise of your own spirit. There is a rising of your own vibration. Please do not belittle the value of praise. Your praise is an expression of gratitude, through some joyous activity. Praise God often. Praise your children often. Use the power of praise to celebrate the wonderful gift of life that elevates you out of any circumstances while lifting you to a higher height.

Praise can also be used in business situations. If you are a supervisor or manager, I pray you are not operating in the fear principles manner. This type of manager spreads fear around as a method to control and manage a group of people. This type of manager is usually poorly trained in management and is spiritually immature. Spiritual immaturity is a life of blame, shame, and fear. No personal responsibility is taken and it is the lowest level of spiritual development.

Verbal prayer can be done in the form of a letter. The following thank you letter that emphasizes spiritual growth in knowledge and praises God for allowing me to love more deeply:

> *Dear Holy One,*
> *I want to thank you for my becoming aware of my natural state. It is believed by me that many people still think that their body is their existence. They are defining themselves incorrectly as a body. I am aware that my true existence is spirit. Spirit is my true identity. Spirit has been further defined as perfect peace, perfect joy, and perfect love. Therefore, I am perfect.*

No longer do I hold myself responsible for the mistakes that I have made as a body. No longer do I blame others for the things that their body does. All of us are spirits. This has allowed me to love you more completely. Since you are not responsible for the things that happen in the human realm, I can love you even more now.

This also means that I have no issues. My sense of fear seems to have resided in this body. Since I no longer identify myself as a body, my sense of fearlessness seems to have grown. There is little or nothing that seems to cause me to be fearful now. For this I am very grateful as I am living a very peaceful existence through this manner of living. My plans are to continue my communication and relationship with the Holy One to further grow in awareness of your desires for me and love you and all more completely. I affirm my innocence and yours.

Yours truly,
Gerald

Five-Step Prayer Treatment
There are many forms of verbal and written prayer. Also, it's important to be aware of scientific prayer treatment. This five-step method of prayer is emphasized in the New Thought Trinity which affects the world around the person praying. Here is a prayer using the five step prayer format.

Purpose: To receive a larger income.

Step One-Recognition: God is abundant and wise. God is the ever expanding universe that is all powerful, and everywhere present. I recognize God as a presence that is all love and loving. It is in the desire of God that we all experience God's love.

Step Two-Unification: Knowing that God's presence is everywhere, I acknowledge my oneness with this presence. Every aspect of God is truly an aspect of me and I accept the abundant nature of God as my right.

Step Three-Realization: I recognize myself as an abundant being that has a wonderful income that provides for me in a plentiful ways. God is the source of this income and it has taken form out of the formless. This large income allows me to meet all my obligations and further my ministerial work without concern or financial worries. I experience the gifts of God when I cooperate with my spiritual life. I share my gifts with pleasure and start a process of continuous giving and receiving.

Step Four-Thanksgiving: I give thanks for all this wonderfully abundant universe provides for me. I receive prosperity and my praise is rich, easy and joyous. For this I am humbly grateful.

Step Five-Release: I release my prayers to the law of provision. The law does not consider nor contemplate; its function is for me to simply obey that which has been spoken and accept its wonderful work. Amen.

Note that the prayer starts with an intention of purpose.

- In the first step there is an acknowledgement of God and an existence that has certain qualities.
- In the second step, prayer unifies you with God.

- In the third step there are the statements of truth that you desire to experience.
- In the fourth step there are statements that show gratitude to God for having answered the prayer.
- In the fifth step, this is the release you receive from allowing the law of God to execute the commands of the prayer. This step concludes with amen which is the final word of release.

Here we speak of the trinity to further explain this New Thought Trinity. The prayer is spoken by the conscious mind and is planted within the subconscious mind. The conscious mind is often called spirit. The subconscious mind is called soul. Body is the creation in form by this planting of the spirit and soul. In the prayer of purpose the seed is the thought of a healthier income. The seed is planted in the subconscious mind and the plant or body is the result that is the improved income. While this prayer recognizes God and the abilities of God, its purpose is to affect the world of effects and bring forth more income. The prayer fulfills a need.

The fourth step is the offering of gratitude for the supply that the fifth step receives. There is nothing the praying person must do to affect the outcome after the release is done. All movement is done in thought. It is not known if the person praying later starts working to assist the universe in some way depends on the level of growth that you have achieved. You make the decision whether the universe needs your help in any way. The author believes that it is best to let the universe do the work and remain open to assist and receive.

Both of the above prayers have merit. Both appear to suggest good things happen for the person praying. God has already provided. No one else is affected by these prayers. However both suggest that the person praying is doing good things for society both in ministry and in love for others being affected.

Please recall the third trinity and you begin to understand that these types of prayers may no longer be necessary. The idea of need, an ego driven feeling may have entered your prayer and now you are looking at the circumstance to fill an assumed lack. *Lack does not exist in the kingdom of heaven.* An alternative is to pray scientifically for eternal matters such as peace or joy. Of course God is not doing anything, other than teaching you how to change your mind set.

Non-Verbal Prayer

Non-verbal is the prayer being done in thought. One can sit in a chair or lie on a bed and think their prayers. One can visit a church and sit near an altar and silently pray as well. Going to a church is of value because of the heightened sense of the presence of God in these prayers. The author believes that God is equally present in all places. There are no places where there is more God than others. We bring our God with us when we arrive at these places. If a certain place looks more pleasant or is known as a place of worship, our prayers may be more effective only because of our mindset in these places.

I find myself more peaceful, for example, when I spend time in parks. There is something about natural environments that seem to settle my soul. Fully aware that God is seamless. I still feel this way about natural environments.

Formal Meditation

Formal meditation takes several forms. There is complete silence where one just goes within and concentrates on their breathing initially. Later one lets go of the breath and has a freefall into God.

Another form of meditation is through repetition. In this form a person repeats a phase throughout the meditation. Such a phrase as "Be still and know I am God" is a good one to use.

This type of prayer can be done in combination of meditation and silence, as you let what happens just happen. This prayer quiets the mind and brings about a peace that is quite desirable. Most notable is that there is no desire to change anything in the world and is achieved by the statement being repeated. For that reason it is considered a beautiful prayer to let God manage everything. This type of prayer allows the Holy Spirit to manage the world. *As this being is made of perfect love, it can manage everything in the world.* Clearly understand that there is no decision that God must make. God is not capricious. Praying will simply continually build faith.

Both of these forms of meditation can be done with eyes closed or with eyes open. One wonderful meditation done in this way is a walking meditation. Just walk through a park and look at things without giving them any thought and attention. In this way you do not control your thoughts. You are letting your thoughts arise and float away. Then the next thought arises and it floats away, this process goes on and on while you meditate.

Living in the Now
God recognizes that your thoughts block you from accessing God. Since God is mind, when you clear your mind you leave room for God. This is done by living in the now. There are essentially two methods of living in the now. Since we cannot live in meditation, we learn to be in constant communication with God by getting our own thoughts out of God's way.

Inhale and exhale right now, as you become conscious of your breathing, you enter into the now. In the moment you leave the world of thought, you gain communication with God

The second method is to pay full attention to what you are doing. This takes practice. For example you have dishes to wash. Before starting, you mentally state to yourself that you shall practice being aware of the presence of God while doing the dishes. Pick up a fork and do not rush washing it. Soon you begin to enjoy washing the dishes. You are accessing and acknowledging that you are in the presence of God, and not concentrating on the menial task of washing the dishes. You can remain in his presence while doing any menial task.

Another way of looking at the practice of meditation is to live deliberately. This means that everything you do is equally prominent and important or nothing is more important than anything else. You are not rushing in the moment to get anywhere. You are consciously living in the now. When you shower in the morning, you say "I am taking a shower," and you focus. Don't let your mind wander, and before you know it, whatever you are doing is enjoyable. Time passes quickly. Emulate this practice with everything that you do. You will find life more enjoyable.

Living deliberately and heavy thinking are not the same. Heavy thinking is an awareness of what one is doing without trying to figure things out. There is focus and there is awareness.

God lives in eternity, and you enter into eternity when you enter the now. It is the space between yesterday and tomorrow. The important thing to remember is that yesterday no longer exists and tomorrow is yet to come. We acknowledge now as a continual moment. It is the only time that exists. There is an eternal now.

I live in eternity by being right here in the now.

We think about what we did yesterday, and this behavior drags the past into the present. We may desire something in the future or we may have fears about what may happen in the future. Yet really, we don't *know* what is going to happen in the future. Living in the now releases the judgments and baggage we have picked up from yesterday. It also releases the future to allow creation and its power to operate in our lives and our future.

Another way of looking at the now is that thoughts block other thoughts. Clearing the mind at least provides more ability to focus. We want the thoughts of God. A mind must be open to let more of God in. Clearing the human thoughts makes room for more God thoughts.

This is the real value of living in the now. Since prayer itself is an act of thought, so as we open to the thoughts of God, we reduce our thought level. This explains why the simple minded live so easily. It also explains why all have access to God because access is not earned. We are always with God. The notion of letting go of our human thinking simply suggests that we experience God more easily when we make room in our thoughts for God.

I received a call one day from my friend Harriet who was visiting her mother in the hospital and she asked me if I could come to the hospital. When I arrived, I stood at the door for a moment watching Harriet giving instructions to the nurse as she stood beside her mothers' bed. Another patient was in a bed close to the window, and that patient seemed to be experiencing some discomfort. There seemed to be a level of stress in the room that caused me to feel an amount of discomfort as I watched.

Harriet finally noticed me and said, "Gerald please come in. I need you to say a prayer right now."

"I feel the need to do something else. How about I sing a chant? This feels more appropriate right now," I responded.

"Just do something," Harriet said.

I had put myself into a position where I should have been very uncomfortable. Harriet was an opera singer with an incredible voice. Did I have the courage to sing in her presence? Normally I would not consider doing such a thing. However, before I enter any hospital room I pray to put myself into another state of mind. Actually, one of the practitioner training points is to not enter a hospital and see sick people. If they do, they should leave the premises. Does this make sense to you? Normally it is understood that if you enter a hospital you will see sick people. Yet this statement has a spiritual meaning.

When I enter a hospital, I take God thoughts with me. God thoughts are beautiful and they lift up the environment. With respect to my singing in front of Harriet, I think about the fact that I have a mind steeped in spirit and not fear. The confidence and faith of such a mind is more spontaneous and just operates in such a manner.

I did a Hindu chant for about a minute. This chant was in the ancient language of Sanskrit. It was a language that I did not expect anyone in that room to understand. Please also understand that I was operating under the consciousness of prayer that was done before entering the hospital. In other words, I was not thinking.

Harriet looked at her mother after I finished and turned to me.

"Thank you. I have been hoping that she would relax so that I could have a break. We even considered giving her some medication to put her to sleep. You have done the same without the medication." I looked at both patients and they were sound asleep. Harriet and I felt a sense of peace.

Through my chanting I cleared a space for God to enter and do what was needed at that time. I did not know the patients needed sleep. In effect, I brought a consciousness of peace into the room and strengthened my own peace while I chanted.

The phrase "clear a space for God," means that God is in my mind. As I clear my mind of thought, peace prevails, and I clearly receive the gift of God as other minds join in the experience.

I spent about an hour there and neither patient awakened during that time. We all know the healing power of a good sleep. My job that day was to bring a consciousness of God into the room. I am always careful that I don't claim credit for anything. God is always creating opportunities for the children of God to learn and be beneficial to others. I am a willing vessel.

Speaking in tongues and chanting phrases in languages you do not understand slows the mind and may bring it to a state of peace. I often cook and look at cooking as a way of staying present. Cooking for me is a spiritual practice. Living in the now is where we meet eternity and God.

The Holy One's Gift to You

There is a gift that the Holy One has for you that strengthening your ability to focus, and focus strengthens faith. The gift that God gives is the spiritual forces that assist you in accomplishing any objective that your seek. This is important because the world has so many distractions in it.

Through this heightened focus you are able to move beyond the distractions. However you cannot move beyond them without a prayer practice and reaching the space of silence. In this silence you experience that peace of God and the oneness of all. It is a space that cannot be described. You must experience it yourself.

Any distractions can be called your forgetting mechanism which causes you to become distracted and forget who you are and what you are doing. Through prayer, practice and study you are present. This requires devotion. *This devotion grows as you learn that you have a deep love for your creator. This is really the only definition of self-love that makes any sense.* As you grow this love in reality you become stronger. Focus is growing faith that can move mountains. As your faith increases nothing is impossible to you.

A somewhat more challenging part of this is when you are called upon to become humble. You are asked to be guided by holiness. It can be a very brief period, but it allows the holy one to demonstrate its love for you. Stay in communication with it through this time. Yet you will be very active. Balance your spiritual practices with activity and have fun. Be joyful as you gracefully move through this period with a newness that is so incredible.

You will be pleased with these gifts. They allow you to understand how important you are to God. Yes, you have enough God to do anything and have so much joy while you are doing life.

You begin to experience visions which are tools that are teaching you about oneness. Do not share them too quickly. Remember to speak to God about your visions and get a clear understanding of what they mean. They are for you. Yet, only Holiness can help you clearly understand them.

There is a Biblical statement in the Sermon on the Mount where Jesus asked that you speak to God in secret so that he can reward you openly. An example of this is a case where I simply told Holiness of some things I was working on.

"Holiness, I hired a life coach" excited that I had hired someone to help me promote my books. Some weeks later after getting to know me better the coach said to me.

"I suggest that you cease listening to your inner voice. I want you to listen to me only and follow what I tell you to do, as best you can."

Later that day I sat down with Holiness. I told Holiness about the conversation I had with my life coach. I was concerned about not listening to my Inner voice.

"He told me that I have to follow his instructions and avoid listening to my inner voice," I said. I did not hear any words from Holiness regarding the matter. That was fine, I know that Holiness heard me and would respond in some manner.

The next day my life coach sent me a text telling me that someone had taken my slot, paying much more than I was paying, so he was going to let me go until further notice.

I believe Holiness was protecting me. I liked my life coach but felt a bit uncomfortable about telling me to turn away from my inner voice. I did not want to make the decision to fire him. He had been hired to help me with my desire to make more headway with my writings. Yet, a decision was made for me. I believe that Holiness has the best answers for me to reach any goal.

Each can and must learn this. There is a section above in this writing that discusses prayer practices. One such practice of treatment is to plant desirables in your mind each day from your conscious mind to receive. Unfortunately the conscious mind holds the ego. Ask for clarity on where you want to go with your life. Most importantly just learn to surrender your desirables to the direction of Holiness. It fully understands. It is also responsive to you.

Holiness wants to teach you the beauty of the mind of Holiness. It does not need your agreement or direction to be holy. It does not take direction from you in an ego state. It simply shows you that it has infinite ways of operating. Be observant and humble. Holiness only wants you to be Holy. It does not need anything. Holiness does not take from one to give to another. It gives and all are lifted in some way.

The Boarding House

Begin to see and understand the choices that are made for you by Holiness. The chapter on prayer a natural way gives you suggestions on how you keep God on your mind. Yet, this section is one of those intermediary steps. It is a repeat, but I suggest that you hear this clearly now.

The ego is still a difficult concept, yet by now you have come a long way. The journey is not complete until you bind the concepts to see your growth. You live in the now state of mind and live a life free from the distractions of the ego. *The now provides a safe haven from the ego.* All of us have learned about our ego and now we must learn to turn away from it.

You are a beautiful spirit being, one with your maker. Anger and such emotions are no longer a part of you. Claiming to be "only human" is not acceptable. You are not human. All of these unpleasant feelings belong to the ego. You are beauty. You are love. You are light. Each is a mind within a great mind.

The history of our planet is the history of the damage the ego has caused. Can you see that by releasing the ego and living in the now you can live in harmony with those you have chosen to live with?

It becomes easier to make the decision to let go of situations that are filled with fear and pain. These emotions are telling us where our work is. Let go with the understanding that you are the one who has chosen not to build another such situation. These are your choices.

However you define it, there are forces that will care for your body and your existence. I teach that love teaches love. God knows how to love. Those forces come to you if you consistently learn that there is one lesson. *The lesson is the fact that the lack of exceptions is the lesson.* You must keep God on your mind and live with compassion. This may be difficult, yet when you practice compassion to your daily life. Everything becomes easier.

I once rented a room from a person who I argued with all the time. She consistently spoke with anger and her words were often not pleasant. She smiled when she spoke, but was really speaking from worry and fear. Initially it was a little confusing to me because of the light smile that really did not appear as anger.

After a few episodes with her I began to soften. I accepted her as a part of my mind and stopped engaging in her conversations. I began to speak differently to her and allowed her to be part of my awakening to the truth of both of us.

In the garage and in her bedroom she bred dogs for money. I had an agreement that I could live in that environment if I could cook in the kitchen without interference from as many as nine dogs and puppies. Fortunately there was a large clean back yard and that is where the dogs spent most of their time.

It was a very large home, and when I heard them barking on occasion, it didn't bother me. I had done a lot of work on myself, but this was a lesson for me.

One of the difficulties I had with her was how cold she kept the house and her constant bickering. I bought a space heater for my room and bathroom, but it was terribly cold in the mornings when I went in the kitchen to cook my breakfast. I even agreed to pay and additional amount for the larger electric bill she had, but that really didn't work for me.

I was angry because I had agreed to pay for something where I felt it was her responsibility to handle it. I kept my space warm and clean during the winter, but now I had to deal with her constant complaining about the rise in the electric bill.

Let's focus on my anger. This was my problem. I did not like the agreement. My ego emerged. It wasn't until I heard her cries and fears after she broke out in tears about the treatment of dogs from a news report she was watching on television, that I remembered my compassionate heart.

She was drawn to me and wanted to talk when I came to the kitchen. Yet her conversation was always the same. Some new report or problem angered her. I began to see without my own ego. She was a blessing, because my anger showed that I still had work to do on me. Anger is not a quality of the spirit I say that I am.

I began praying privately for my living space so that I could continue to live in that environment. I did enjoy living there and had reached a state where I had to learn that I could not run from my ego. I wanted to take a stand.

I had a few conversations with her about spiritual matters and how we should view and treat one another. She was not the problem. I was not using the gift of Holiness. In order to improve this situation one evening I simply asked Holiness for help with the problem of being in the cold all the time.

Having found my heart and having moved away from my ego, life in that house improved. This woman who was at one time perceived as a problem to me became a good friend.

When you speak to someone in an attempt to change their mind about something you are usually wasting your time. Yet, through prayer you are communicating with Holiness. What is the real difference here? Well, when you speak to another they usually have their ego out front as a defensive mechanism. When you bring your ego, nothing changes. Ego wants to battle. Its primary method is to divide and conquer.

Please give up trying win over someone else. Humility happens when you let Holiness handle the difficult situations in your life. Someone once said to me that "Holiness does the heavy lifting."

Holiness brings the other person into a better state of mind. This is one of the miracles of Holiness. These miracles have no limit. You have no ability using your persuasive techniques. Leave it to God!

Practice, Practice, Practice.
Let us not leave love awaiting you.
Fill the space love has left for you.

CHAPTER ELEVEN

Summary and Conclusions

The vital qualities of life come alive as I learn more of what I am capable of. The capacity to judge something as good or bad diminishes as the healing power of love brings peace, joy, and sets me free from the blinding effects of chronic judging. I have learned to let life be. It just loves.

Within me there was a prompt to write a book about the Holy Spirit. While writing there was assistance given and new ideas began to flourish. Research and inner prompts produced this document. A real difference is made by having an intention and starting to do what was suggested. God makes all things possible. It is not necessary to have certain things in my head when the heart already knows. The need was continual entry into the heart. This does require practice.

Many admire and even worship the person who was named Jesus. Yet, can you imagine having the same teacher he had? Worship and praise are actually reserved for God. Here is your direct relationship. In the Bible book of Mark there is a passage that states that one can actually not prepare and allow Holiness to speak for you. This passage states as follows:

...neither do ye premeditate, but whatever shall be given you in that hour, that speak ye for it is not ye that speak, but the Holy Ghost[14].

The above message is suggesting that you be more spontaneous and open to Holiness. Move away from heavy thinking. Consider the following:

The mind that created the problem cannot and really has no interest in fixing it.

The conscious mind has too much ego within it. You therefore cannot be your own teacher. You are to fire yourself as your teacher and accept your internal teacher. *Accept the Holy One.*

Some time ago I recall writing myself a letter. In that letter I tendered my resignation as my own teacher. Formally I accepted the Holy One as my teacher at that time. You may also decide to write yourself a letter. Most importantly, do not attempt to be your own guide. Most of us have already been converted to the world's way of thinking and cannot guide ourselves. This is the point of the chapter on your total dependence on God. You cannot by the prior definitions of "you" teach yourself. You are totally dependent on God for your teaching.

Accepting this dependence you acknowledge the Holy One. Yes, it is dependence. Yes, it can be called slavery. Yes, it is a wonderful way of living.

This feminine power, of course, can do things as well through you. We are saying here again that this is your master teacher and master lover. Mastership is something that you can attain. You actually become an active aspect of the cosmos.
There you have it. You can grow spiritually beyond all expectations if you just allow the Holy One to

take you there. This is one of the primary tasks of the Holy One. There is little you can do without this being. Actually you can do nothing on your own. The Holy Spirit rarely asks for anything. Simply, you are to maintain stillness. While I do maintain that I was guided to this writing, this was my choice. You may have a higher purpose and choose something else. Writing is one of my ministries.

The Trinities and the Ego

The three trinities were explained and forms of prayer were shown. Use the spiritual science trinity to plant appropriate ideas in your mind. Understand the Christian trinity to understand that you have this wonderful companion and understand who you are in this trinity. The third trinity is where you understand that your mind must heal.

Stay present to be in constant contact with your source. God already knows. These thoughts need not be planted in your mind. God already has the proper perspective of God's child. *Gain this perspective. This is your ticket to the party.*

Gaining an understanding of this term ego is an objective of this writing as well. The ego lives in a state of fear and may cause you to live there as well. Everyone in human form has created an ego. This comes with the belief in human forms. The opposite of fear is love. Therefore the ego is a state of believing that love does not exist.

If you listen to the ego too often it has an ability to take you as its hostage. In this way of living you could spend enormous amounts of time seeking to solve problems. As its hostage, a person is often troubled and life can become unbearable. Illness is a result and finally physical death ensues.

The primary difficulty many have is the inability to recognize the real problem. Having ego thoughts are the problem. Too focused upon the physical is often the problem. Life is spiritual. Scripture says to worship God in spirit and in truth. Your real life awaits you. *Focusing on the problems as if they are real as opposed to ego creations simply magnifies the problems.*

The solution is really one of ignoring the ego problems and placing the attention on aspects of God. In other words gain an interest in something else. That something else must be a creation of God such as peace, that something else is intangible. *The problems will then disappear into the nothingness from which they came.*

Ernst Holmes a famous mystic once wrote:
"If you learn to take you attention off your problems your problems will grow feet and run away."

Another way of say this is: "Where attention goes energy flows."

Through prayer practices putting your attention on the spiritual you place your attention in appropriate places. You put energy where it will do you some good.

Certainly one must clear the streets if a car is coming in their direction. This means that I take care of my body and am attentive to my Holiness. Only those things at my doorstep get immediate attention. The future is in the hands of Holiness. I am perfect for the opportunities that arrive at my doorstep. My long salt baths and bodily workouts that require a stretching of my members to allow retention of range of motion necessary for physical strength and agility assist in the care of my body. I also seek to eat well. While I take care of my body and seek to just ignore problems with appropriate attention, my main work is with Holiness.

It takes spiritual courage to do this. As problems may seem to literally "come out of the woodwork," it takes courage to ignore them. That courage is your faith in truth. That courage is given you by the Holy One. It is faith in God. It may seem too simple, yet anyone interested in spiritual growth must gain this trust in the truth. *It is simply a process of purifying the mind. For some of us it can become a full time job.* Invest your time wisely. There is nothing wrong with becoming devoted. You are simply learning that it is within your thoughts where true change is made in you.

Can you also understand that this process itself may have pitfalls? This process of spiritual growth can take place with pain and incredible creation taking place simultaneously. No need to hold back. Growth happens without pain as well, yet with spiritual growth there is enormous impact upon other lives.

At your creation (note, not at your birth) you could have said "God is." Guess what? That is still true today. That will never change in spite of what your five senses tell you.

God has already made up God's mind. God has already responded to the ego with creation of the Holy Spirit. God does not battle with the ego nor does the Holy Spirit. Neither should you. God assists with the release of the ego and spiritual focus.

You can learn to hear Holiness. This is not really done with ego tools. The ego tools are the five senses. You are to begin to live in the now and not allow your past to be your teacher. Holiness is to be your teacher. Experiences of the past are the world's poor learning tools. This is a poor teacher for anyone seeking spiritual growth. Holiness has a voice that you hear from within. In actuality, this voice does not commonly come forth. Yet you are being guided if you really desire to be guided.

Since God is love, if you are operating in fear you have created a state where you believe that God does not exist. It is your beliefs that need to be placed in proper perspective. Believe in love. In order to return to love you simply seek to fall in love with God. This is done through praise and worship.

At one time I thought that the children of God who grow spiritually become more powerful and their minds become more sensitive to the negativity that appears to them. I am now sure that the child of God must simply learn to laugh more often. They then do not absorb the ugly that is in the world. They are safe.

I understand that when I look at someone operating from their ego, I am looking through my ego. Only an ego sees an ego. I also understand that I must not make the ego a constant area of study. It is unhealthy to study it too often. It is important that we understand it to distance ourselves from it.

God beams with love. You are to learn to beam with the love of God or you may create more of that which you really do not want. Children of God are courageous beings. This is because they know that they have the company of the cosmos. They are being carried. They often work, but without strain. They work for the kingdom and live in the kingdom. The ego is silenced, but as a small part of me, I must include these thoughts as a part that I must learn to care for as well.

Praise and Worship

You see, God has no need to accept your praise or worship. *God has no ego.* You need to feel this praise and worship to return your mind to that state of love. This erases fear and returns you to the state of gratitude. The feeling of gratitude is a feeling of love.

This love that you have has powerful friends that you will attract by having this as your primary state of mind. Since all thoughts take form in some way, they bring such forms as situations and circumstances that you will enjoy. For example this is how you will bring happy friends and acquaintances into your life. This is how you will erase the friends that fear brings. These unpleasant circumstances simply are not created by a person who loves God and seeks to keep such thoughts in their holy mind.

It is difficult to blame anyone for the circumstances of their life. Praise simply asks that the person begin to rise out of situations and circumstances.

Blame is without merit. Praise whatever comes as God inspired and watch for God's friends. These are heavenly thoughts. Your worship brings this level of thinking and these friends that you want. Worship is also stillness. Grace is given entry. *The seamless space of heaven is what you experience.*

Many who worship God are called seekers. They seek to have a greater experience of God in their lives. There is a point in time where the seeker must become clear. At some point they must be clear that they have God. No longer are they seeking anything. They become clear that God is forever present with them. They usually achieve this through their desire to just have the peace of God as their constant companion. You have God now. Just seek to be more aware of this. *The kingdom of God is everywhere and you are experiencing it.*

A behavioral view was provided to show that the study of mind is how one can affect behavior. Viewing the workings of mind is viewing behavior from the proper perspective. One can attempt to view the behavior of animals and that of humans and attempt to gain a better understanding of how minds work.

Since there is really only one mind and it is entirely consistent in its workings, just attempt to study it. Then one has taken a journey into the workings of the final frontier. Working on behavior alone is working from effect and not cause. Mind is cause. Each of us must heal our minds. *You through the Holy One can begin to dominate your physical world by training your mind. In this way you work on cause not effect.*

Be careful as the depth of mind is endless. Forgiveness allows you to let the truth be so. Do not get lost in mind and thought.

A Walk through the Heart

Note that this may seem to be a psychological study when discussing the universe. We have discussed in many ways the ego, which itself is described as a mental creation. Yet since we suggest that we live in the mind of God, we study God, the universe and creation itself by a study of the mind of what we believe to be God's greatest creation. Until a point I believed that mankind was God's greatest creation. Actually, this great creation is the Christ. This Christ is the spirit of humankind. Of course this is simply the Christian concept of the spirit of man. There are many concepts of this spirit and all can be correct if they believe that the spirit is natural love.

Of course it has been stated that God did not create man. Remember, God-created things last forever. *God created a being that is a spirit that seems to be human.* We love and care for our bodies. We simply do not limit ourselves to these bodies by remembering our true existence. This writing suggested that many including the writer at one point tend to put too much emphasis on the physical. In this remembering the mind is purified and the heart is given full sway over thought. *Yes, life is found through that heart space.* As stated, the heart knows. No need to create another mind.

Just recall that the physical world is an illusion. Your body is part of your experience of the physical world. It is illusion as well. Do not ignore it. Take care of it, but remember primary work is in one's belief system. Just remember who you really are.

While it is understood that emotions are powerful energy currents, they wear out the body if allowed to go unchecked. Many are afraid of their own emotions, which they may claim to be an energy of God. Find peace and find the primary energy of God. Here you can enter the Kingdom of Heaven as peace is a primary condition of the Kingdom. It is a Kingdom because it is a place where a King rules. You can become that King for your world. Desire that without ego motives and let these powerful forces come to your aid.

Letting God is allowing the reality of grace to occur. Grace is the expression of God as a love act without our working or planning it. Grace is wonderful, magical, and mysterious. As spirits we operate in an eternal sphere of grace. Grace is also wonderful, magical, and mysterious. Let grace teach you of its magic. *Stay present without the wanting of things and grace becomes your dominate way of living.*

You may have noticed several areas where "no thought" took place. You literally allow the presence of God to be present by moving your "human thoughts" out of the way. You must be careful that by a consistent level of prayer you are strengthening your consciousness. Your creative abilities are also being clarified. Therefore, as you pray you must stay in the now more often and/or think about God more often. Thinking about spirit may be achieved through having a passage of spiritual import pass through your mind many times a day. In this way you become an incredible beneficial presence.

Information was provided on the natural way of communicating with God. Several ways of maintaining this communication were reviewed. Prayer has many forms and you can choose the form you choose to provide room for this channel. Prayer is an act not just a study. It can become a way of living. It is a wonderful way of living. While dependence upon it can seem weak, nothing is further from the truth. Through prayer you receive your "daily bread" and find energies that cannot be fully described.

Learn of gentleness and innocence. These have nothing to do with age. Here I learn and experience life without any suffering. Pain is impossible. The gentle are safe. The gentle are innocent. The gentle are kind. Joy in inevitable.

The most appropriate communication with God is not through words. It is best done with complete silence. It is a space that cannot be described. For in the silence everything disappears and only God exists. You will only understand these words if you have experienced this in the past. Otherwise, just await it. It is truly heavenly.

Be very careful about too quickly telling others about your conversations with God. You can lose much energy by attempting to communicate something that was intended only for your use. God will communicate with the others. You are to just demonstrate your love for God and your connection through your living. Your attempts to communicate that intended for your thoughts only will only confuse you and often the listener. Let God be God. You know how to do this!

Your life is about the threefold way of being. You are to pray, practice, and study. The most important aspect of this is practice. Practice believing that all there is God. This takes practice because the five senses will seek to teach you otherwise. However, if you believe this, all you can do is begin to practice believing it. For it is true. *God is literally every-*

where and within all things. We simply learn to get out of the way. We are giving up ego dominance. We are realizing our true existence as wondrous spirits.

The seamless space of heaven is here now. I had an experience recently where thoughts were just racing through my mind. I was attempting to meditate. My call was to the Holy One to help. Suddenly, I took a deep breath. My body seemed to just heave without my thinking about it.

Yes, this breathing was my gateway to now. I then began to focus my attention on my breathing. Continued to breathe and let the thoughts just flow into that space where my breath just left. Calmness ensued. Here I was in that space. This is so simple. Who wants to complicate this? Just be.

Doing this appropriately is really the easiest thing you will ever do. This is because Holiness asks for nothing. Opportunities emerge, yet they will be done for you with proper attention. The seamless space has no holes and no otherness. Simply there are no impediments. Just a march forward by a universe that is progressive by nature. This progression is the outer. The inner does not change. It is already completed. Again it is difficult to understand where there are no obstacles. *Your part is willingness and devotion.*

What is devotion? It is willing yourself to do your spiritual practice consistently. You are not to criticize yourself or your practice. You do not evaluate yourself. You are to just practice.

Little attention was given to service and your life as a giver. Yet this cannot be avoided when Holiness is directing. It happens under the direction of Holiness. Through these acts of kindness, the soul which is said to be invisible becomes visible as you.

You have no idea of the level of peace and infinite joy you can experience when letting this ego go. When Holiness is present, this ego dissipates. Prove to yourself that you are not an ego and do this by keeping Holiness present. Do not allow others to become your source for ego support. You do this by accepting that they are whole.
Your eyes will seek to tell you something else. Do not believe them. Have faith that God is everywhere. Nothing needs to change. You need simply

to accept that God did a good job. This means that you just have faith that all is well.

It was stated that by giving you learn more about what you already have. It is therefore necessary that you become a giver. The outer world is a world of exchange, but its purpose is shown to you by your giving freely. That is, it is teaching you what you already have. *Specifically you have everything.* Therefore you can give with no thought of loss.

My five senses are being trained to see as are yours. You are so appreciated. Note this is your feminine. All of us have this feminine side. It is gracious. Has nothing to do with male or female. Each of us can access this side. The masculine is to just be observing.

We learn of Holiness by perceiving properly and that comes with vision. There is a Bible statement that says that *"without vision the people perish."* Let Holiness bring proper vision to you so that you can see your eternality. Yes, you are an eternal being.

You did nothing to create spiritual laws. You can do little to learn of them and operate efficiently within them short of asking for help and beginning a study. As you ask, it is given to you. This writing is considered to be a companion work to the book entitled _The Only Life Worth Living_. Bringing your newfound knowledge to the spiritual practices of that work is a wonderful combination of how to live a life. You soon learn that nothing is impossible to you and the Holy One.

Absolutely all things are possible. A seamless flow just is. Holy forces are absolute. You get to practice being an aspect of this absoluteness. This is really learning what is already true about you. Much of this work is simply letting things be. The truth is all around you. Seek to be an observer of it.

The language of Holiness is often not in words, but is largely symbolic. Whether you hear a voice or not, trust that you are under Holy guidance and care.

Holiness does have an interpretive function. It does interpret the words and operates on them. There are metaphysical teachings that allow one to read with an eye to symbolism. Holiness has this power and interprets what is passing through your awareness at all times.

A brief story is coming to my attention right now. After moving into that boarding house where I rented a room, I noticed that one of the persons who lived in the home was an older Korean woman. There were times when I had difficulty understanding this woman because of her accent, but I began to understand that she was experiencing some pain.

She told me that she was taking high doses of vitamin C and garlic to attempt to rid herself of a tooth pain that she was experiencing. At this point she also told me that she was allergic to penicillin and could not take this to relieve the infection in her tooth. The dentist who she could not continue to pay had told her that one of her teeth was infected.

"Would you be open to a suggestion from me to assist your ridding yourself of the pain?" I asked.

"I am interested in anything that helps me," Lucille said.

"I have had difficulty sleeping the last few days as this pain is so intense and I have been awakening throughout the night to take a pain medication."

"I have heard you speak of some financial problem as well that is occupying your thoughts, is that correct?" I asked.

"Yes," Lucille said.

"I suggest that you find something to do to bring you to a state of peace so that anything you take for this pain can work in your favor. The body does not operate well under a state of fear or stress. I will also bring up your situation in my evening prayers," I said.

Later that evening I noticed Lucille sitting in the family room knitting. Several colors of yarn were in her lap as she sat there knitting.

"This will bring me a greater peace of mind and will kill two birds by providing me with a gift for a friend of mine when I finish this scarf. Knitting helps me relax," said Lucille.

That evening I prayed for Lucille in my room. I asked that she be relieved of the pain in her mouth and that she experience a heightened level of the peace of God.

The next day Lucille greeted me in the kitchen.

"The vitamins have really begun to do their job as my pain had completely gone away," Lucille stated excitedly.

"I am glad that you are better," I said.

Lucille did not even consider whether the improvement had anything to do with my prayers. In fact three months later I asked her about the tooth. She told me that her tooth continued to be pain free. She never acknowledged anything I suggested as being helpful. Her lack of acknowledgement is fine. She could not be a good roommate in her pain-filled state. We both benefited.

You must become aware that Holiness is everywhere. You have it as well as its power within you. This is the gift that God has given you that you must accept. Do not ignore God's gift. You will be very happy with this gift. Receive it and be happy. This is the portal we are building together. This portal reaches from the infinite into finite form. You can decide to enlarge this portal for all of creation by your seeming personal spiritual practices. Assume your place in the universal and eternal sphere of things by doing your work on this channel. It is like a radio channel that humans have. This is how our personal world is spiritualized. Nothing is really personal given oneness.

What is being said in many ways is that now you are a healer. You can heal all situations by just allowing Holiness to be where you are. You do this by saying to yourself that you have Holiness where you are. Holiness does not try to heal, it is always successful. When you even see something that is distasteful, just take another look, be willing to allow yourself to remember Holiness and there you have it. Holiness is there.

Be willing and tell Holiness that you are willing to see and you will see things differently. You may also have some interesting mystical experiences. Now you heal and become healed.

The body cannot make itself sick. The body is completely neutral. Only the mind can become sick and project this sickness into the body. Change your mind. The mind heals as it is more focused on spiritual matters. The body then resumes its place in health and willingness to do the work for which it exists.

There is one power. You are an effect of that power. All effects of God are powerful and wonderful. All God can do is good. It only knows how to be God. Heal minds with your willingness and allow the earth to change. All will find your beauty and you will be in demand, but do not seek popularity. That is not your function. You are a healer. At least you have the ability to bring Holiness. It heals. You are available to just be where Holiness takes you. No difficult decisions, no difficult choices. These have already been made for you. Just be present and let the reality of grace occur. Nothing is impossible to you. Pray and love. Give and receive love. That is all you are now capable of. Awaken to truth! An infinite frontier is before you. A life that is infinite is before you. Love life.

Peace and blessings!

CHAPTER TWELVE

Please Listen!

All of my children have access to me. This is not a debate, it is fact. No one in any way is far from me. This is because I occupy all space and at all times. You who live in time must become aware of my actions and be willing to know that I operate in and out of time. Yet all of my most direct communications are out of time. To you, they will seem to be dreams and will seem without meaning. Yet, all that I do has meaning. Do not be so sure about your interpretations. Leave that to me. I will assure that you get my meanings.

Everyone is my child. This is because all that is exists within my space. Humans, though, are one of the most evolved and thus must be given special consideration now. Yet, human hood is just an appearance. *Everything is truly spirit. There is nothing else.*

Come to me my child. Come open and empty. Let me fill you with my love and learn to let go of yours. Mine will satisfy you and let you know of your wholeness. All my creations are whole. You therefore can drop your doubts, fears, and inhibitions and aggressively move with me. Be humble before me and be sure as you do my will. We do have one will and that has been explained to you. I can speak loudly and I can speak softly, yet I can and do speak to you.

Learn of me and learn that all that I have is in you. Within your heart is everything necessary for you to know. You only need to learn anything if you feel lacking in some way. Lack will never be true. All that I create has my essence which is wholeness.

Take good care of what you consider your children, yet know that you as parent are simply my caregivers and vessels for my will. Your children contain the same innocence that I have placed within you. I guarantee your innocence. I also guarantee that there is no limit to your mind as long as you agree not to limit me. My mind is also in you and therefore there is much you can ascend to.

Do unto your children as you would have them do unto you. I will always place mirrors in front of you and you will therefore be able to see all that you are by looking within this mirror. This will be someone close to you. Love them. This may be someone you seemingly hate. Love them. This can be the worst sinner you can imagine. Love them.

You therefore love yourself within this mirror. Thus, love yourself. *This child is you. I only have one.* To your eyes what seems to be many is one. Make it one and you return to heaven while seemingly within a body.

Some of my children speak of needing more self-love. Love me and you will find yourself loving yourself more completely. This simply means that you cannot grow self-love through loving what you have been erroneously taught about yourself. You grow self love by becoming a being of love within your mind. This is because the truth about you is spirit. Spirit is love. You are therefore to learn to love everything.

This is one of your choices. Yet it is not a choice I have given. I have given one choice. That choice is heaven as you have called it. Time is only there for you to eventually make this choice. It is the only one that assures your return to me. Make it now. There is no need to lose anything, yet it will be easier if you renounce your imagined need of anything. Let go of it all and heaven will stand before you in its brilliance. You are literally this heaven. I have built it to protect you and you have no way of exiting it.

How could you ever exit yourself? The very fiber of your being is me. My child, please just allow this fabric of my love define you for you. Teach yourself these lessons and you teach truly. Teach only love.

You have the ability to become a messenger of my love wherein you first receive the message for yourself and share it. The mirrors have messengers that can become yours. You can then practice speaking my word and my voice will speak through you. All the channels are mine. Learn that I am always with you and you will understand that looking back I was always with you.

Do not become confused about the order of receiving my message and becoming a messenger. You will soon see that giving my love is how you receive more of it. The lesson is that you cannot out give me. I am an infinite resource for you to draw upon. I never deny you. I love you.

Hear the message that you must keep me on your mind. You cannot stop your creative ability. Therefore you must think about the good or learn to stay in the now. Do not misunderstand the importance of this message. The health and happiness of that body we share depend upon it.

I am as close as you believe or seemingly as far away as you believe. Allow yourself to have me on terms that are favorable to you. Let yourself fall so deeply in love that you experience truth. *I have everything for you. Take it. Never cease to make broad demands upon me. I implore you. I will never cease to give and receive all that you choose. Just let love be itself.*

Begin to talk directly to me. Yes, just begin to talk. I will hear you. I will also respond to you. Yet, do not put too much emphasis on what appears to be my voice. I will respond. *I never ignore my children.*

Become aware of that term guidance. You have and must be willing to accept divine guidance. This may seem weak and ignorant. Yet many have taught of the bliss of such ignorance. It is really a true power. Use it.

My teacher is within you. These are also my children. Beautiful child of God, do not concern yourself with how your children come. I will bring them. Bring yourself. Bring your friends. Bring your mates. Come! You will be glad you did. You will also learn that this is the only environment where you can be truly happy. *You were not created to believe that you can live outside my love.*

Yours truly

EXHIBIT ONE

A Story of Gratitude and Manifestation

Some years ago I was on the phone speaking with my earthly father. I was in Los Angeles and he was in Chicago. I noticed a hint of sadness or concern within his voice and became curious. "Dad, I detect a hint of concern in your voice. Please let me know what is on your mind," I said.

He responded, "I am impressed by your listening skills. You detect a troubled person right now. I have found myself in a financial bind and do not see a way out."

"I recently received a $5,000 credit line that I could borrow from and I would send that to you if you want,"

"I really do not want any more debt at this point."

To which I replied, "You are my father. I will borrow the money and you need not even think about paying me back. I will give it to you. It was a mistake to tell you that I would be borrowing the money."

After a few minutes, he said, "Let me think about it son. I will call you to let you know shortly."

The next day my dad called me to say that he would take the $5,000 and would pay me when he was able. I told him that I would send him a check and that he was not to concern himself with paying it back. I remember a sense of feeling very good about my ability to help my father and immediately sent him a check for $5,000.

I was so **grateful** to be able to do this for my father. Since I knew that it was a Thursday and the check would probably get to him on Saturday, I didn't immediately get the credit advance. Since the interest rate on the advance would be high, I decided to wait until Tuesday of the next week to get the advance. That would save me about five days of interest.

Over that weekend, my ex-wife came to me with another problem. She and I were separated because of a drug addiction that she was experiencing. We had tried several drug treatment centers; however none of them had worked. It had finally dawned on me that she would not respond to any treatment until she was ready and we had simply lived apart until she found a way to free herself of that addiction.

The problem she brought to me was a check that she showed me in the amount of $35,000. This was a cashier's check made out to her. Since it was a cashier's check I knew it was good and wondered where she got it.

"Please tell me where you got the money from. I cannot deal with any drug money," I said. She responded, "This is not drug money. I was a caregiver for an elderly woman for a year without pay. You know how well I cook. She needed money for another purpose and took out a mortgage on her property to give me this money and it was a small portion of the money she borrowed."

The problem she faced was that her bank had refused to cash the check for her. She told me that she would give me a portion of it if I would help her cash it. Since it was a cashier's check drawn on her bank, this made no sense to me that she would have difficulty cashing this check. Upon entering the bank with her on that Monday, I noticed that the guard looked at us a little strangely.

When we got to the teller, I was given a further explanation of the problem. I was told that my ex-wife had thrown a fit in the bank on Friday when they refused to give her $35,000 in cash as she had asked. They explained to me that someone has to make an advance request if they desire to withdraw that much cash from a bank on a given day. The branch only keeps so much cash on hand and was unwilling to give that much cash to her without an advance notice.

The branch manager had pulled me aside to tell me this story. I then explained to my ex- wife that they could give her a lesser amount in cash and place the balance in her checking account.

At that time I could envision what had happened days earlier. My ex-wife was probably excited to have money available to her and was angered when she was unable to get to it. Through her anger, they were unable to give her an explanation and she had been escorted out of the bank by the security guard. This time she deposited the check in her account, and withdrew about $3,000. She had them give me a check for $8,000. We then left the bank all smiles without any difficulty.

"I hope that I have made some amends to what happened to our marriage. Please continue your care of our only daughter and let her know that I do love her," were her words.

This was the same woman who decided to clear out all the funds from two of our joint checking and savings accounts when she left our household. I had lived with her addiction for some years and had been counseled by her mother to put her out of the house to get her away from our daughter. This was the counsel of my mother in law, but I was unable to just leave my wife on the streets. Her mother had told me that I was an enabler. This I had also learned from a counseling center I had visited. I enabled my wife to do drugs and financially supported it. Of course, I learned this the hard way. This was a painful lesson, financially and emotionally. She did leave our home and left me with a nine year old daughter to raise.

Later that day I when depositing the check in my account, I noted that I would not need to get an advance from my line of credit to provide the money to my father. Somehow this money had come to me with more to spare without any effort at all. I was in awe of the situation; however it is here that my point about giving ideas away can be explained.

My willingness to give to my father with love must be understood. Gratitude is a feeling of love. There was no hesitation. I was joyously willing to give the $5,000 to my dad. I distinctly remember the joy I felt when mailing the check to him. This joy, which I characterize as love, was the cause of my wife bringing the $8,000 to me. I had spent much money in the past helping her and paying for the drug treatment centers; however that may have been her reason for giving me the money. Yet, I am aware that my willingness to share with my father was the reason it came to me.

The lesson here is that one must be willing to share with love, which is a feeling of gratitude. Give your love away and watch it come back to you in measure and ways you cannot imagine. Be **grateful** that you are able to share.

Remember that the universe will respond to your willingness to give with a sense of **gratitude**. We do not get to say where it will come from nor can we say the amount or texture. It could be money or whatever our real need is. Just understand that the universe is monitoring your thoughts. Have your thoughts be thoughts of gratitude. This is what a universe of love wants to feel from you. You will enjoy its response.

Consider creating a gratitude journal where you daily list the things that you are grateful for. List things that you have and those you desire to experience having. In both cases the universe is listening. To the degree that you can accept it, the universe will gladly take the form of whatever you can believe you have and are grateful for. Be it health, money, or whatever your desire, express gratitude for it. Do not forget to express gratitude for that which you already have. It is the pleasure of the universal father to grant that which you graciously accept.

EXHIBIT TWO

Meditation Topics
& Prayer Practices

This is a seven minute meditation where one is asked to meditate on a set of words or phrases. It is generally called contemplative mediation. Use each topic a day at a time. No concern about being too ritualistic. Vary your prayer life and you find a great deal of satisfaction with it. Meditations are to be short to avoid the habit of allowing the mind to wander often. Be certain through journaling or just talking to communicate with Holiness each day.

Meditation Topic #1
There is just one power.
God is the only power and presence in the universe.
There is just one.

Spend the first three minutes repeating these words. Then spend the following four minutes just concentrating on your breathing and sitting in the silence.

Meditation Topic #2
I live in a world of love.
There is nothing here, but love.

Love is all there is. Spend the first three minutes repeating these words. Then spend the following four minutes just concentrating on your breathing and sitting in the silence.

Meditation Topic #3
I am grateful for Holiness.
I live in gratitude.
I am grateful.

Spend the first three minutes repeating these words. Then spend the following four minutes just concentrating on your breathing and sitting in the silence.

Meditation Topic #4
I live in a world of peace.
There is nothing here, but peace.
This deep calm is what I am.

Spend the first three minutes repeating these words. Then spend the following four minutes just concentrating on your breathing and sitting in the silence.

Meditation Topic #5
The meek shall inherit the earth.
Gladly I join in meekness.
Gladly I am among those who inherit the earth.

Spend the first three minutes repeating these words. Then spend the following four minutes just concentrating on your breathing and sitting in the silence.

Meditation Topic #6
I am the Christ

I am the whole Child of God
All power and all life have been given to me

Spend the first three minutes repeating these words. Then spend the following four minutes just concentrating on your breathing and sitting in the silence.

Meditation Topic #7
Everything is just as it should be
I let the truth be so
I rest in peace

Spend the first three minutes repeating these words. Then spend the following four minutes just concentrating on your breathing and sitting in the silence.

There will come a time when you will decide to release time with respect to your meditation. Consider just entering meditation. When you feel you are complete, let yourself stay a few minutes longer. You will enjoy this. Especially in the presence of others begin to monitor what comes out of your mouth. Do you quickly join in the naysayers doom machine? Consider about a week of this monitoring and above all, ask God for help. God can assist in keeping you in that high altitude of a good attitude. This is another of those ego hampering practices. Be aware of your mouth as it can defile. Consider a prayer on your growing fearlessness. Yes, with God which is always true, you are fearless.

Prayer and/or meditation topics:
- Peace
- Love
- Joy
- Innocence
- Gentleness
- Eternality
- Divination

Take a piece of scripture such as "Be still and know I am God" as a thought that you allow to go through your mind for a full day or days. Meditate on this. Consider that this is one way of practicing being in the now and not allowing your mind to fall too long away from its source. God is all you are and of absolute necessity. It is your mind that is being purified of stale thought.

Lengthen your morning and/or evening prayer times as you desire. Yes, this is the mind work. Remember your spiritual guide and its power that it gladly shares with you.

Glossary of Terms

Abundance —A large quantity of anything. Be it money, clothing or relationships, anything or things in a large quantity.

Affirmation —Statement to restate or say yes in agreement with something stated or desired.

Avatar —The appearance or incarnation of a deity on earth. May refer to a guru or any revered being.

Bless —Constructive thought directed at anyone or anything.

Bible —The sacred book of any race or group.

Body —Anything that is seen, heard, touchable, or smelled in the manifest universe. The physical universe is all body.

Christ —The creation of God that each may seek to reach in mind and acts.

Communion —Make mental or spiritual contact with God such that minds become one. It is a listening within to the stillness.

Consciousness —Mental awareness. The entire knowing within a mind.

Conviction	-Compelling awareness of anything.
Divination	-Make divine or the act of declaring everything divine.
Ego	-The part of the mental awareness that hold belief in what has been seen or experienced. This is the part that believes itself separate from its creator.
Error	-That which is not true. A mistake or erroneous act.
Eternal	-That which last forever. Something with no beginning or ending has always been and will be forever.
Feminine Principle	-That which is the eternal soul. Sometimes referred to as the womb of nature.
Forgiveness	-Look past or let go of. Filled with the ability to forgive.
Grace	-The givingness of spirit. That which is received without personal act to get.
Groundedness	-Dwelling in the moment.
Heaven	-That part of consciousness that is all God. Each is literally in heaven at each moment.

Holy Spirit	-The creation of God in response to the ego emergence. A being that is fully God who has the task of clarifying and making all knowledge divine.
Human Training	-The common training that parents or the world provides to a being. Often considered to be socialization and of value.
Idea	-A mental concept.
Illumination	-Conscious contact with the divine where one has reached a state of brightness that is divine.
Illusion	-An image that is not considered to be real. A creation of mind that is not eternal.
Instinct	-A feeling that may sometimes be considered primary in the nature of a being. In an animal it is considered to be the ability of such animal to be directed to its needs. In humans it may be considered to be a divine inspiration.
Issues	-An emotional response to data or an act. A person is said to have issues when they respond emotionally to a set of circumstances. Considered to be a frailty of a being.

Jesus

-The name of a man who is believed to have achieved Christhood. This person unified himself and thought with God and became the Christ.

Judgment

-A view of something that may be an opinion or way of viewing something. Spiritually this is considered to be negative as it is assumptive.

Kingdom of Heaven

-A part of mind that is fully controlled and ruled by divine forces. Filled with beauty and joy this is a state of mind that is also filled with peace and therefore blissful.

Lack

-A state of being without.

Law

-That which maintains order. There are laws of the divine and there are laws of the physical. One is a higher law and enables actions that belie physical laws.

Light

-That which enables seeing.

Manifest

-Bring into form. Make believable.

Mental

Clouds	-That in mentality that blocks light and possibly love such that abilities are weakened.
Mind	-That which has thoughts and ideas.
Neutral	-That which is neither negative nor positive.
Praise	-Give great ideas to or heap great compliments to. It is said that praising God is healthy.
Prime	-First in order. Primary refers to that which is first cause.
Rampage of Appreciation	-Spending time writing or recounting the things that one appreciates. Making a list is one way and listing minor as well as major items.
Religion	-A system of thought of a group or race. Often referred to as the consistent acts of a being. Such as to do so religiously or often.
Sacrifice	-Give up in order to receive something else. Often referred to as a loss taken to obtain something greater. In this writing we state that the Holy Spirit never demands any sacrifice.

Science   -The ordered laws and principles that go-
                   vern a system.

Self
 Realization   -To become aware of one's true self.
                   Awakening to what is one's nature.

Spirit   -That which is not seen but believed to
                   animate beings.

Universe   -All of creation.

Whole   -God. All are considered whole whether
                   they know it or not. For all is God.

Will   -Refers to a decision coming into execu-
                   tion. For example the will of God is
                   something that must occur.

Word   -The ability of spirit to declare itself into
                   manifestation. All of creation seen and
                   unseen is the word of God. We do not
                   consider any book or text to be the com-
                   plete word of God.

Reading List

Below is a recommended list of books that add to and possibly support the teachings of this book-God's Holy Spirit.

Author	Books
Eckhart Tolle	The Power of Now Stillness Speaks A New Earth
Joel S. Goldsmith	The Foundation of Mysticism Invisible Supply The Art of Meditation
Ernst Holmes	The Science of Mind This Thing Called Life Effective Prayer
Howard Thurman	For the Inward Journey With Head and Heart
Anthony De Mello	The Way to Love
John Selby	Seven Masters One Path
Julia Cameron	Blessings

Gerald E. Collins — The Only Life Worth Living

Foundation of Inner Peace — A Course in Miracles

Unity Publications — Metaphysical Bible Dictionary

Christian D. Larson — The Pathway of Roses

Michael B. Beckwith — Spiritual Liberation

Neale Donald Walsh — Conversations with God

Brother Lawrence — The Practice of the Presence of God

References

1.   Cannot serve God and mammon.
Holy Bible Matthew 6:24

2.   No man cometh unto the father, but by me.
Holy Bible John 14:6

3.   As thou hast believed, so be it done unto thee.
Holy Bible Matthew 8:13

4.   For in him we live, move, and have our being.
Holy Bible Acts 17:28

5.   The test of perfect peace. A Course in Miracles,
Foundation for Inner Peace Publications

6.   Definition of the Christ. Science of Mind
Textbook a Devorss Publication

7.   But, lay up for yourselves treasures in heaven.
Holy Bible Matthew 6:20

9.   Blessed are the meek, for they shall inherit the
earth. Holy Bible Matthew 5:5

10.   The Father that dwelleth in me, he doth the
works. Holy Bible John 14:10

11.   I have overcome the world.
        Holy Bible John 16:33

12.   The Pathway of Roses by Christian D. Larson,
        Newcastle Publishing, Inc.

13.   Stillness Speaks, Namaste Publishing and New
        World Library

14.   It is not ye that speak, but the Holy Ghost.
        Holy Bible Mark 13:11

15.   If they do not free themselves from their mind
        The Power of Now by Eckhart Tolle

Author Biography

Gerald Collins became a licensed Religious Science Practitioner at the Agape International Center in Los Angeles, California, in 1997. Michael Bernard Beckwith, founder and spiritual director of Agape, taught Gerald as his minister and class facilitator. Mr. Collins has spent over 15 years teaching universal spiritual principles to children and has been an assistant teacher in Agape's University of Transformational Studies and Leadership. Gerald has also spent many years studying and facilitating A Course in Miracles. He considers this course to be an important aspect of his thought system.

Since 1976 Gerald has been a professional teacher and financial manager as a Certified Public Accountant with a Masters' degree in finance. Mr. Collins has written for a children's magazine and has been a contributor to Inner Visions, an Agape monthly publication since 1997.

His first book entitled *The Only Life Worth Living* was published in May, 2009. Since that time he has written five additional books including this one. He is an avid reader who has dedicated himself to studying the lives of mystics in the world's wisdom traditions, a practice which has greatly impacted his own spiritual life. All of his books, blogs, and additional material for thought can be found on his website which is geraldcollins.com.

CPSIA information can be obtained
at www.ICGtesting.com
Printed in the USA
FSOW03n1717170816
23827FS